Praise for

A Walk with Jane Austen

"A young woman goes looking for Austen in all the places Austen once lived and many of the places she wrote about. The Austen she finds is a woman of family and of quiet but sustaining faith. Austen shares these things and many others with author Lori Smith whose book gives the reader the great pleasure of time spent with both. A lovely, intimate read."

—KAREN JOY FOWLER, best-selling author of *The Jane Austen Book Club*

"Sensitively written and carefully paced, this memoir takes the reader on a tour of the author's experiences while journeying around England in the footsteps of Jane Austen. Lori Smith moves seamlessly from romantic daydreams, through a close questioning of her relationship with God, to battles with her mental and physical health. The book reads as an intimate and honest memoir and has enough to satisfy the non-Christian (like myself) if they choose to look beyond the somewhat unexpected (in a mainstream book at least) pairing of Jane Austen and Christianity. Above all else, this is a book about searching—for love, meaning, peace with oneself, health, a good night's sleep, and a decent cup of coffee that wasn't made with that freeze-dried instant powder—and these are experiences that anyone of any faith can relate to.... A welcoming read. Lyrical and questioning...perfectly pitched."

—EMMA CAMPBELL WEBSTER, actress, author of *Lost in Austen* and founder of lostinaustenblogspot.com

"In this engaging, deeply personal and well-researched travelogue, Smith (a *PW* contrib   f Jane Austen's life and wri   . Readers will learn plenty   and intimate circle of family and friends, her candid letters to her sister, her possible loves and losses, her never-married status, her religious feelings, and her untimely death at the age of 41. But it is the author's passionate connection to 'Jane'—the affinity she feels and her imaginings of Austen's inner life—that bring Austen to life in ways no conventional biographer could. Smith's voice swings authentically between her own raw, aching vulnerability as a single Christian woman battling a debilitating and mysterious chronic illness and the surges of faith she finds in the grace of a loving God. And yes, Smith even meets a potential Darcy at the start of her journey. This deliciously uncertain romantic tension holds the book together as Smith weaves her own thoughts, historical research, and fitting references to Austen's novels into a satisfying whole."

—*PUBLISHER'S WEEKLY* starred review

"With wit, charm, and rare honesty—of which I have to believe Jane Austen would have thoroughly approved—Lori Smith weaves her personal life experiences throughout her journey into the life that was Jane's. Infused with faith, romance, loss, and a search for self, *A Walk with Jane Austen* makes for that rare book that keeps popping into one's thoughts and beckoning one back."

—TAMARA LEIGH, author of *Perfecting Kate* and *Splitting Harriet*

"With deep and sometimes heartwrenching honesty, Lori Smith weaves her story and Jane's together into a wholly unique narrative. In the midst of a craze for treating Austen's novels as little more than glorified bodice-rippers, Lori brings to bear her perspective as a single Christian woman who can identify in many ways with Austen's own beliefs and experiences, exploring truths and ideas that others gloss over. The resulting book stands out like a beacon."

—GINA R. DALFONZO, editor of The Point Weblog and writer for BreakPoint Radio

A Walk with
Jane Austen

A Journey into Adventure, Love & Faith

Lori Smith

WATERBROOK
PRESS

A WALK WITH JANE AUSTEN
PUBLISHED BY WATERBROOK PRESS
12265 Oracle Boulevard, Suite 200
Colorado Springs, Colorado 80921
A division of Random House Inc.

All Scripture quotations, unless otherwise indicated, are taken from the New Revised Standard Version of the Bible, copyright © 1989 by the Division of Christian Education of the National Council of the Churches of Christ in the USA. Used by permission. All rights reserved. Scripture quotations marked (KJV) are taken from the King James Version.

Details in some anecdotes and stories have been changed to protect the identities of the persons involved.

ISBN 978-1-4000-7370-2

Copyright © 2007 by Lori Smith

Illustrated map by Devin Boyle copyright © 2007

Published in association with the literary agency of Alive Communications Inc., 7680 Goddard Street, Suite 200, Colorado Springs, CO 80920, www.alivecommunications.com.

All excerpts from *Jane Austen's Letters,* collected and edited by Deirdre Le Faye, reprinted with permission of Oxford University Press.

Library of Congress Cataloging-in-Publication Data
Smith, Lori, 1971–
   A walk with Jane Austen : a journey into adventure, love, and faith / Lori Smith.— 1st ed.
   p. cm.
   Includes bibliographical references.
   ISBN 978-1-4000-7370-2
1. Austen, Jane, 1775-1817—Homes and haunts. 2. Austen, Jane, 1775-1817—Influence.
3. Novelists, English—19th century—Biography. 4. Literary landmarks—England. 5. Women authors. 6. England—Description and travel. I. Title.
   PR4036.S63 2007
   823'.7—dc22
   [B]

                                        2007025455

Printed in the United States of America
2007—First Edition

10 9 8 7 6 5 4 3 2 1

for mom and dad

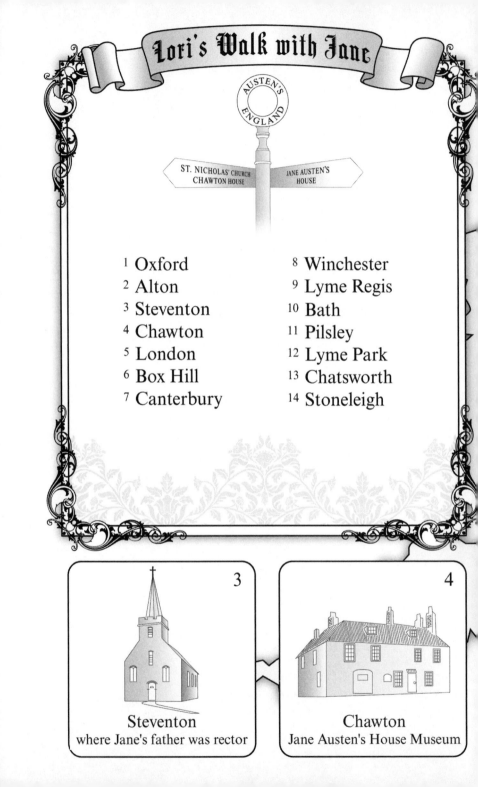

Lori's Walk with Jane

AUSTEN'S ENGLAND

ST. NICHOLAS' CHURCH
CHAWTON HOUSE

JANE AUSTEN'S
HOUSE

1 Oxford
2 Alton
3 Steventon
4 Chawton
5 London
6 Box Hill
7 Canterbury

8 Winchester
9 Lyme Regis
10 Bath
11 Pilsley
12 Lyme Park
13 Chatsworth
14 Stoneleigh

3

Steventon
where Jane's father was rector

4

Chawton
Jane Austen's House Museum

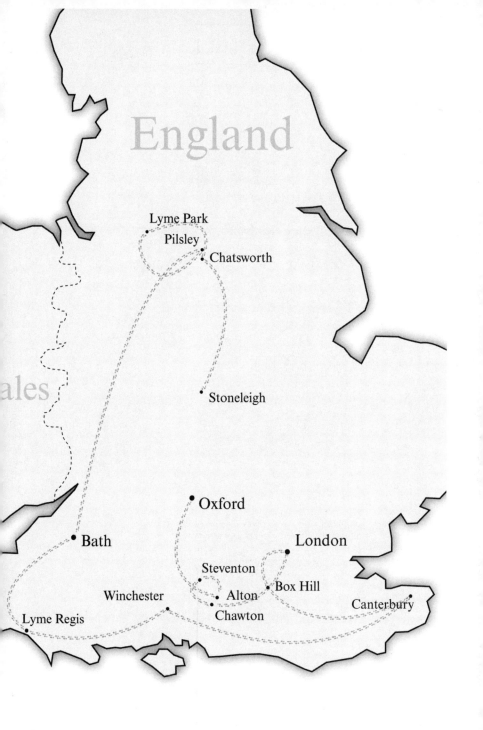

Lori's Walk with Jane

This guide will help you track (and trek through) the places Lori visited on her pilgrimage in the footsteps of Jane Austen—where Jane lived and loved.

Oxford

St. John's College: Jane's father, George, and brothers James and Henry attended St. John's; it was founded by a distant relative of Jane's mother. www.sjc.ox.ac.uk.

Christ Church Cathedral: Both George and James Austen were ordained to the deaconate here. www.chch.ox.ac.uk.

Wycliffe Hall: Where Lori attended summer school. www.wycliffehall.org.uk.

Hampshire

Alton Abbey: Where Lori stayed. Dom Nicholas is an expert on Jane Austen and leads occasional Austen retreats. www.starcourse.org/abbey.

Steventon: Village where Jane grew up.

St. Nicholas, Steventon: George Austen was rector here. www.dutton.force9.co.uk/nwsadhs/stevchur.htm.

Ashe: Village where Jane's friend Anne Lefroy lived. www.ashevillage.co.uk.

Jane Austen's House Museum: Also known as "Chawton Cottage," this is the house Jane lived in with her mother and sister on her brother

Edward's estate. She wrote or edited all the books here.
www.jane-austens-house-museum.org.uk.

Chawton House Library: This was Edward's house in Chawton, now a
library for the study of early English women writers. Tours of the house are
offered. www.chawtonhouse.org.

Hidden Britain Tours: Offers Jane Austen tours of Hampshire.
www.hiddenbritaintours.co.uk.

London

Box Hill: Setting for the picnic in Emma, now a National Trust property with
hiking trails. Roughly an hour from London. www.nationaltrust.org.uk.

British Library: Has Jane's writing desk and glasses on display, along with a
manuscript copy of *Persuasion*. www.bl.uk.

National Portrait Gallery: Contains the pencil and watercolor sketch of Jane
by her sister, Cassandra. www.npg.org.uk.

Covent Garden: Jane's brother Henry's banking business and home were for a
while at 10 Henrietta Street.

Canterbury

Godmersham Park: Edward's estate.

Goodnestone Park: Edward's in-laws' estate; he lived close by at Rowling for a
while after his marriage, and Jane and Cassandra visited him there.
www.goodnestoneparkgardens.co.uk.

Winchester

Winchester Cathedral: Jane is buried here. www.winchester-cathedral.org.uk.

8 College Street: This private home behind the cathedral is where Jane and
Cassandra came to stay while she was being treated by Mr. Lyford. Jane
died here on July 18, 1817.

Lyme Regis

Jane set parts of *Persuasion* here—readers will recognize the Cobb and the Granny's Teeth steps. www.lyme-regis-dorset.co.uk/.

Bath

Jane set parts of *Persuasion* and *Northanger Abbey* here and lived here with her parents and Cassandra for several years after her father retired.

Jane Austen Centre: A wealth of information about all things Jane. www.janeausten.co.uk.

Roman Baths: Visitors—like Admiral Croft in *Persuasion* or Mr. Allen in *Northanger Abbey*—often came to "take the waters" at the baths, which were thought to have healing properties. www.romanbaths.co.uk.

Pump Room: Jane's characters visited the Pump Room to walk and drink the spa water. You can still drink the water here or stay for dinner, as it's now a nice restaurant. www.romanbaths.co.uk.

Beechen Cliff: Catherine hikes Beechen Cliff with the Tilneys in *Northanger Abbey.*

Assembly Rooms: Jane visited the Assembly Rooms for dances and concerts, as do her characters. The Museum of Costume is now on the lower floor. www.nationaltrust.org.uk and www.museumofcostume.co.uk.

Villa Magdala Hotel: Where Lori stayed. www.villamagdala.co.uk.

Derbyshire

Jane set Darcy's home—Pemberley—here, though she likely never visited herself.

Lyme Park: Pemberley in the 1995 BBC version of *Pride and Prejudice,* with Colin Firth and Jennifer Ehle. Now a National Trust property. www.nationaltrust.org.uk.

Chatsworth: Pemberley in the 2005 Focus Features version of *Pride and Prejudice,* with Keira Knightley and Matthew Macfadyen. www.chatsworth.org.

Devonshire Arms Pub, Pilsley: Where Lori stayed. Also, great food. Many pubs in the UK only serve lunch, but proprietors Rod and Jo Spensley give occasional "carvery dinners." Phone: 01246 583258.

Stoneleigh Abbey

Jane's mother's family's estate. Jane came to visit with her mother after her father died. www.stoneleighabbey.org.

Contents

PART 3

In which I stumble upon deeper meanings of grace.

A Note on the Text

*Those who tell their own story you know must be
listened to with caution.*

—SANDITON

Many friends and acquaintances who first read portions of this book on my blog were under the impression that perhaps the story was fictional or were at least confused enough to have to ask. So since the veracity of memoir is generally questioned these days, I feel compelled to say that this is a work of nonfiction. Everything I report about my life in the following pages actually did happen.

I am indebted to several Austen scholars—particularly Deirdre Le Faye, whose painstaking research has been invaluable in sifting out rumor versus fact in Jane's life. Biographers agree that there are gaps in our knowledge of Austen. I've tried to note wherever I am assuming or imagining what her life may have been like. Any errors are entirely my own.

There is only one aspect of the text that is semifictional, and that is that I did not write it in its entirety on the trip. I kept a detailed journal but didn't have the luxury of being able to write out all of my thoughts at the time.

Memoir is a subjective art in that it always comes back to your perspective—not only your worldview per se, but also your emotional stance toward the world. If you simply related facts as they happened, and related every available fact, you would have an incredibly unread-able and uninteresting book. We don't choose what happens to us, but I suppose we choose (even subconsciously) how we remember it and what stories we tell.

Admittedly this is my interpretation of what happened—filtered through a lens of humor and grace, always with an eye for getting as close to truth as possible—along with my favorite stories from Jane's life. She would never have written a book like this herself—she didn't even keep a journal that we know of—and I think she would have been horrified to be the subject of one. But she might have found inspira-tion here for one of her own intelligent romances. No doubt she would have had enough material.

Loving Austen

*If adventures will not befall a young lady in her own
village, she must seek them abroad.*

—NORTHANGER ABBEY

I've always loved Jane Austen. Or perhaps it would be more correct to say that I, like so many women, think Colin Firth as Mr. Darcy is the ideal man.

I didn't start reading Austen until I was in college and picked up a copy of *Pride and Prejudice* at a used-book sale somewhere. I still have the copy, the bluish-green cover with two desolate watercolor women on the front who look like they belong more to Brontë than Austen. I read it over Christmas break at my grandparents' house in Sacramento. I was there alone, waiting for the rest of the family to get in, when we would all drive down to L.A. for my brother's college graduation.

But before that, I was there with Grammy and Bob, my step-grandfather, in the simple house his uncle had built in the fifties for eight thousand dollars. It still had the green shag carpet then, the green sofas, the lovely yellow kitchen with gold-patterned sheet-vinyl floor with brown spots in the crevices that wouldn't come out. In later years,

Grammy would turn up the heat at night until it was stifling, and Bob would end up in a wheelchair, unable to maneuver. Grammy and I would come back to the house to horrible excretory smells because Bob had trouble making it to the bathroom alone. The laundry sat dirty in the bathtub, and Grammy sometimes forgot to change clothes. I couldn't stay with them then, but on this trip they were still young-old, and I was sleeping on the Murphy bed in the guest room. I stayed up late after they went to bed, smelling comforting old-house smells and reading *Pride and Prejudice,* greedily turning pages, awash in the glory of unexpected love.

I was in full-on crush mode at the time, the kind of simple crush perhaps that can strike only an evangelical college girl at twenty when she has yet to be kissed. This particular crush had Austenian themes in that, like Elizabeth with Darcy, I wasn't attracted to the guy at first, until I got to know his character and figured out what a great guy he was, and suddenly he became terribly attractive to me.

So I followed Elizabeth and Darcy, dreamed of my own unlikely romance, and fell in love with Austen.

⚜

What's not to love? Jane Austen was born into a house full of love and activity on December 16, 1775,[1] in the village of Steventon, to a father who would soon be leading prayer services against the American rebels.[2] George Austen was rector at St. Nicholas, a small stone church built in the 1200s[3]; he hid the church key in the trunk of the old yew that still guards the churchyard.

Jane had six brothers and one dear sister, Cassandra, who was always her closest companion. Her parents ran a small farm, along with a boys' boarding school in their home. Her mother loved to write sharp, merry poems, and her Oxford-educated father could teach all of his children (but especially the boys) whatever they needed to know of Greek and Latin. There were family theatricals in the barn, with lengthy prologues written by the eldest brother, James, and a strong network of family and friends who visited often and might stay for months at a time.

The Austen home seems to have had a sense of abundance, though the family's finances were not certain, at least when the children were small. George regularly borrowed money and then borrowed from a different source to pay back that debt, so there was a constant juggling and never catching up, though not for lack of very hard work.[4]

The world at large was chaotic, ships firing on each other broadside in the name of war, and plenty of war to be had for England—with the colonies, with Napoleon, throughout Europe, North America, India, and the West Indies. George III was on the throne going mad, to be replaced by his obnoxious, licentious son, George IV, as regent, laughingly known as "Prince of Whales."

It was in the noisy house, in the quiet village guarded somewhat from the chaos of the age, that Jane began to write.

⁂

To me, Jane Austen's books (and the movies based on them) have become the entertainment equivalent of comfort food, what I return to over and over again when I need a break from the real world, when I need to retreat. I've watched and read them so many times. Once, flat on my back with a four-month-long exhaustion that my doctors could only describe as "a mono-like virus," I pulled out my VHS copy of the BBC version of *Pride and Prejudice,* only to find that I had worn out the pictures and was left only with sound. I watched five hours of gray static that time, listening to the voices and music, imagining the scenes in my head.

But after years of reading and rereading, I began to feel like I had nowhere left to go. I knew the plot lines of Austen's books and was familiar with the corners of her fictional world. But I knew little about her life. I wanted to know the stories that made her who she was, the things she never wrote about, the characters of her family and friends, her navy brothers.

I read Carol Shields's biography and Claire Tomalin's *Jane Austen: A Life.* I was thrilled to find Austen's own witty and at times caustic voice in Deirdre Le Faye's collection of her letters. I read her brother Henry's biographical sketch about the sister from whose pen "every thing came finished"[5] and her nephew's glowing memoir about the aunt who, in his mind, conjured her romantic stories solely from "the intuitive perceptions of genius, not from personal experience."[6] I wanted to see the Hampshire countryside, the old Norman-era church where her father had been rector, the site of the rectory with the hill Jane rolled down as a child, like Catherine in *Northanger Abbey.* Lovely Bath, where Jane stopped writing for so many years, taunted my curiosity, as did the Cobb at Lyme, the houses in Derbyshire on which she may have based Pemberley, her brother's huge estates, the small cottage in Chawton where she sat to write in the room with the squeaky door so she could put her work away quickly if anyone disturbed her.

And that is how I found myself in the middle of a Hampshire wheat field, alone and nearly lost, on a sunny day in mid-July.

PART I

In which I go to Oxford and fall into something like love.

One

Crossing Oceans

*I do not want People to be very agreable [sic], as it
saves me the trouble of liking them a great deal.*

—JANE AUSTEN IN A LETTER TO CASSANDRA

It's actually an uncomfortable thing to pursue one's dreams,
however attractive they may sound. Perhaps this is why most of
us only *dream* dreams and never live them. For several years I have tried
to err on the side of taking risks to live the life I want, to do the things
I feel must be done. But there is a creeping, stealthy anxiety that has
wound itself around me in such a way that I cannot escape, even here.
So here I am, alternately anxious and pinch-myself-I-must-be-dream-
ing thrilled.

I am wearing ugly hiking shoes and have decided I don't want to
go to England, which wouldn't be such a problem if I wasn't at forty-
one thousand feet somewhere south of Greenland, headed into a month
of following Jane Austen's life through the country.

Also, I'm in a mood for falling in love, which is its own kind of
malady. Meeting loads of interesting people—one of the initial attrac-
tions of this trip—now seems painful, and I'm sure I would be far more

comfortable at home with a good thick book, and I'm sure Jane would agree. Jane did not like to be forced out of her familiar circle either. Perhaps the people I meet will not be terribly nice or intelligent to save me the trouble of liking them much.

If I could manage to fall in love without having to actually meet someone, that would be ideal.

My friend Kristine talks about "crowded rooms," as in "one day you spot a stranger across a crowded room" and everything changes, and I think the Oxford classroom I'm headed for may be crowded in that sense of the word.

And part of me believes in the mystical and mysterious—and wacky—just enough to think that, because I'm an Austen devotee following in her steps, perhaps she will deign to craft a little romantic comedy of my own, in real life, from beyond the grave (which seems absolutely ridiculous on paper, but there it is). Funny that these little thoughts we barely acknowledge become hopes or beliefs.

Plus, I suppose, as a single woman there is always the expectation that *if* you are going to meet someone (not that you have to, but *if* you are going to, and it seems right somehow to imagine this happening in your life), it *should* be now, because time is getting on and all and now we are thirty-three (and who could have ever imagined that we would be thirty-three and single?).

Of course, my friends were glad to help me ponder the possibility of a whirlwind British summer romance while acknowledging that it would be completely unnecessary to the outcome of the trip—but wouldn't it be fabulous, if, you know, you never know when you might meet someone, and I am going to be in *England* after all—home of Colin Firth in all his shirt-dripping glory. (Except thanks to Bridget

Jones we now know that Colin Firth actually lives in Italy, for all his traipsing about the English countryside in movies.)

Actually, the Austen story may have begun with an Oxford romance. It's thought that this is where Jane's parents first met.[1] George Austen, around thirty, was finishing a divinity degree at St. John's and working there as assistant chaplain. Cassandra Leigh visited her uncle Theophilus in Oxford from time to time. Cassandra may have known George the way everyone else did, as "the Handsome Proctor."[2] And Cassandra's wit and beauty must have gotten his attention.

What we know for sure is that George and Cassandra Austen married in Bath shortly after Cassandra's father died[3] and seemed to have loved each other deeply. Neither had much money. Their eight children (they never adopted the regularly used birth control of separate bedrooms) and bustling home were a reversal of fortune of sorts for George and must have been a great comfort to him. He had been orphaned as a small boy and then kicked out of his father's house by his stepmother, eventually taken in by an aunt until he landed with a scholarship in Oxford.[4]

Generations of Austen men followed George to study in Oxford— two of Jane's brothers and several nephews—preparing for taking orders in the church, which was kind of a family tradition. (One of Jane's nephews even proceeded to take orders although his wealthy great-aunt had threatened to disinherit him—just one of the signs that the Austens were earnest and sincere in an age in which the church itself was largely corrupt.[5]) I will be there for a week-long theology summer school and then traveling through southern England for three more weeks.

Oxford is not the first place people think of in connection with Austen—the Hampshire countryside or Bath readily come to mind—

but if Oxford is where George and Cassandra Austen fell in love, perhaps in some ways it is the best place to start.

So I am dreaming of romance and trying to expect nothing and afraid of it all the same. My suitcase weighs forty pounds (including roughly twelve pounds of books), my backpack another twenty (ten pounds of shampoo?). Roughly two hours' sleep last night. Bad hair day. Hoping I do not get a blood clot and die of DVT or collapse from hunger and starvation. It's a difficult, romantic thing to be a dreamer.

***

I've always felt a kinship with Jane (and the biographers tell me I should always call her Jane Austen or Austen but never Jane, which is far too familiar)—a closeness many of her readers wrongly assume. She feels like a dear friend. Could we meet her, though, she would no doubt find the ridiculous in us, wherever it lurks. And whether intensely private Jane would want to talk to any of us is up for question.

People ask, "Why? Is it the romance?" The truth is, I don't know exactly. There are all kinds of reasons. And, yes, it is the romance (*but only partly,* she says with great pride). Poor, intelligent women. Rich, full-charactered men. Happy endings.

In some ways, this trip is about sorting out the possibilities of my life, working and dreaming to ensure that sans husband and children, I will still somehow be significant. Oxford, grad school, studying theology—these are things I have dreamed about as an avenue to meaning, an answer to the unexpected aloneness of my journey. In this feminist age, it is slightly annoying that it still at some level comes down to that, to being alone and wishing I were not, to wondering a little now and then what to do with myself.

So, yes, I love Jane in no small part because I love Darcy and Knightley and Wentworth. But there is so much more to Austen. (There is so much more to me, as well. For example, I happen to be poor and intelligent.)

Austen's writing is full of wit and energy; she is ready to find and laugh at anything ridiculous. C. S. Lewis wrote of her "cheerful moderation."[6] G. K. Chesterton, in the introduction to a 1922 edition of *Love and Freindship* [sic], one of Jane's juvenile stories, wrote:

> These pages betray her secret; which is that she was naturally exuberant…her original passion was a sort of joyous scorn and a fighting spirit against all that she regarded as morbid and lax and poisonously silly.[7]

In the midst of her light stories, Austen seems to have captured some essential, unspoken truths about who we are and why we do what we do. Hers are characters in the truest sense of the word, in that their motives and desires are exposed, moral victories and failures on display. No thought or action is too small for Jane to relate if it will help us accurately make out a character's, well, *character.*

I am curious about her faith, which evidences itself in a gentle way in her writing. And I wonder about the difference between her books, with their sweet romances, and her life, in which she was disappointed in love and widely regarded to have rushed herself into middle age.[8]

Ironically, though now unbelievably popular, Jane lived a small life. She wasn't so much hemmed in by her Hampshire countryside and family and steady group of friends as she was at home in her quiet routines, her thriving simplicity. I don't know when the suspicion began for me, but for a while I've had a growing fear that my own life is small, when I crave bigness. I would like to make a grand contribution to the world to justify my existence and help define me. What thrilled Jane makes me panic. I don't want to be small. I want to be incredibly, unbelievably significant. (And yet could anyone accuse Jane of being insignificant?) I know that part of that is good and spiritual—this desire for a life not to be wasted—and yet it seems a great stroke of pride.

I hope that somehow this proximity to Jane's life will help me understand my own.

⁂

In some ways, those of us who love Austen look to her to escape into another world. When our own is complicated and stressful, hers is tea and careful conversations and lovely dresses and healthy country air. (Which, of course, is a great oversimplification of the time in which she lived. Nonetheless, that is what we find.)

And that is part of my hope for this trip. Or rather, I have already begun to reinvent my life, and this trip is part of that.

I suppose I should say that for all the laughing and half-serious musings about whether or how Austen might manifest herself on this trip, there is another, bigger part of me that is consumed with trying to manage my anxiety.

I sit here on the plane as an escapee of depression. When depression has followed you for a while, when you have begun to leave it behind, it's difficult not to feel that it may still be stalking, may pounce again at any inopportune moment.

A year ago, in the middle of the workday, I started to cry uncontrollably and had to leave the office, realizing with sudden clarity that I was in an emotional pit, that the depression that had been mildly following me for a few years was now nearly complete and all-encompassing.

As my brother would say, when you find yourself in the middle of a catastrophe, it's likely because there's been failure on multiple fronts, and that was the story of my depression. Over several years there had been spectacular tragedies and slow deaths, things I thought I had assimilated. There were multiple fault lines running through my life, encouraged by an overwhelming, numbing exhaustion. I could no longer hold all the pieces together enough to make it feel mostly good. It was mostly very bad, with a dead end–ish, hopeless cast.

It all started, I think, on Labor Day several years ago. I was nursing what I thought was a cold, only to end up in the emergency room at 3:00 a.m., bizarrely unable to swallow even my own spit my throat hurt so badly. (I still felt like a wimp showing up at the emergency room check-in saying, "My throat hurts.") They gave me Tylenol with codeine that I could barely get down and a thick numbing gel to swallow, which made me throw up. I went home and rested and saw my doctor but didn't get better—for months I was exhausted, with a low-grade fever, attempting to work part-time but mostly not able to work. The dishes piled up all over the kitchen counters; the laundry was too large a task to comprehend. This was that mono-like virus. The doctors couldn't diagnose the exact strain but assured me that although it might take me six months to get back to work, I wouldn't be permanently impaired. I am afraid they might have been wrong.

I went back to work full time after four months. The fatigue lingered in spite of my determination to will it away. I developed life-altering insomnia. If I was able to get to sleep, chances were I would wake up and feel as though I hadn't slept at all, as though my body refused to rest. I walked about semicatatonic, attempting to suppress my out-of-control emotions, trying to go through the challenging daily rituals—getting up in the morning, getting dressed, getting to work on time (a near impossibility), doing something productive, making dinner. Batteries of tests showed nothing substantive that could be causing the problem, so exhausted me tried futilely to get more sleep, to go to dance class with my lethargic muscles. I was ever hopeful that things would once again be normal but forgetting what normal felt like.

Work haunted me; there were days I drove to work in tears. It's a familiar, soul-killing story. I was given responsibility without authority, held accountable for things I had no control over. I had to deal with aggressive co-workers whose superiors washed their hands of the situation. In this case, the organization was a large Christian nonprofit, and the mismanagement was all in the name of God—which to me was devastatingly sad. Before that had been the self-absorbed, near-compulsive-liar boss who slandered my reputation as he shoved me out—also, of course, a Christian. I knew in my head that none of these was entirely or even largely my fault, but I was contaminated with insecurity.

It had been years since I'd felt at home in a church—since my family group, the Bible study group that I worshiped with and backpacked through Grand Canyon and Glacier with, had fallen apart. None of us was comfortable anymore in our church, the church I grew up in. We still firmly believed but had developed a distaste for the trappings that came with faith—the obligatory political conservatism, the focus on church involvement over engaging the world, the guilt trips, the failure to understand or appreciate artistic approaches to truth. We called ourselves "The Inquisitors" after the Dostoevsky story that was one of the first our reading group tackled and because we were all about asking questions. In retrospect, the name was ironically apt. We judged the church harshly and went in search of new ways to express our faith and, in the process, bickered and lost each other.

I felt unmoored. I found a new church. I went to a singles' Bible study with dreadfully long hours of teaching. I continued to go on Sundays because my faith—my relationship with God—was incredibly important to me, but I felt like I couldn't relate to most of the people there and wondered if they could understand me—sad, struggling to believe.

I longed for a life outside the stuffy, often sickly sweet, and sometimes nonintellectual spirituality of the evangelical Christian world. I hated that I had gone to a Christian college, worked for Christian organizations. I began to feel that any group of professional Christians would provide unexpectedly stellar examples of incompetence and, at times, pure meanness. I wanted out. I desperately wanted to go back and rewrite my life—to go to a state school, get a master's degree, study abroad, survive in the "real" world.

I had not married. As a somewhat conflicted semifeminist, I had dreamed of and planned for and wanted marriage since I was a lanky, brown-skinned girl winning faux beauty contests at friends' birthday parties. I ached for the meaning and compassion a husband would provide, for the chance to make my own family.

Everything in my life was dark, stifling. I needed light and air.

If nothing else, I knew I could be brave. I went to counseling. I gave myself permission to feel the badness of it all. I reached out to friends.

I learned things about myself that I didn't want to know—that I could be passive-aggressive (when you try to stuff away your emotions, they have a way of leaking out elsewhere), that I was holding other people responsible for my emotional well-being. I decided to give myself grace and determined to change.

I went to a specialist, who found a thyroid imbalance that had been kicked off by the virus four years before. He gave me a prescription, and very slowly I began to feel better. I got more rest and had fewer lost days.

I saved thousands of dollars and determined to leave my job and write for a year, to see if I could make it. I started going to an Anglican church that I love. I started to date again—a blind date, a guy I asked out, a guy I asked out because he wouldn't stop talking (always a bad sign), a friend who flew up from Atlanta. I was out of my comfort zone in so many ways, forcing myself to engage with the world again, to try. Within six months, if not a new person, I had at least worked my way into a new perspective on life, with hope and possibilities, with a more independent me I rather liked.

In January I gave my notice. In February I walked away from meetings and coffee breaks and lunch breaks and paid vacation and health insurance to the gloriously terrifying world of writing full time.

I felt like the jasmine plant in my sunroom that nearly died from lack of water and then sprouted blossoms on dead-looking branches. There I sat, blooming—having willed my way into a new life, having stepped off the cliff into freelance hell only to find it daunting but very, very good. I was still terrified. But I loved life. Like blossoms that were completely unexpected.

Oxford: Dirt and Dreaming

Have you seen any pleasant men?
Have you had any flirting?
—LYDIA, *PRIDE AND PREJUDICE*

The smell of exhaust fumes immediately transported me to Paris. There was something about being young and stepping alone out of the Metro and smelling what I could only identify in that moment as the scent of *joie de vivre,* all the refined activity of the gracious city with its cafés and little dogs, glorious museums and wide boulevards.

My first experience of Oxford had felt dark and oppressive. I looked through the windows of the bus from Heathrow, hoping for signs of romance and spires, but felt only heaviness.

Today dawned sunny and seventy-something—perfect—and my backpack quickly began to stick to my T-shirt with sweat as I headed south, down Banbury Road into Oxford's city center. There are thirty-six colleges in Oxford, and college buildings, chapels, and quads are spread throughout the city, a jumble of imposing buildings interspersed with more commerce than I imagined. Broad Street and High Street and Cornmarket are lined with shops—sandwich places, mobile phone stores, fast-food joints, bookstores, tourist shops.

While in college, I'd visited Cambridge once with my parents. I'd been studying in a little beach town on Spain's Atlantic coast—a difficult trip where eight of us stayed with an American family whose marriage seemed to be breaking (or had already broken) and whose house was torn apart, mid-remodel. I remember a half-finished stairway to the second floor, construction debris everywhere—Sheetrock, nails, plaster. The roof was open. The husband slept on a mattress in the mess. Our teacher slouched along with his Mexican accent and got angry with me for drinking *tinto de verano,* which is just Sprite with a little wine. (Our Baptist credo precluded any kind of alcohol.)

I had yet to master the art of bathing suits that looked good on me, or style in general, and spent four weeks with the awkwardness of trying not to be awkward in a foreign country, compounding my sweet-smart, somewhat-unsophisticated-and-insecure persona. I was cowed at the prospect of not knowing what I wanted to do with my life. So when my parents met me in Madrid for a short European tour, I was alternately thrilled to see them and moody-mean.

I hold in my mind a little-visited string of wonderful memories and embarrassing moments from that trip. My parents and I rode a gondola over gorgeous Barcelona's evening lights. We sat in a street café drinking red wine, in pain after walking around literally all of Paris (my mother was most in awe at the self-cleaning bathrooms at the Arc de Triomphe). In Scotland, we struggled to find a tiny fishing village someone on the plane had recommended to me, and when we did arrive there, discovered it to be, well…tiny. I was embarrassed at the time because of my parents' solid American tourist mentality. *They aren't even attempting to be good Europeans,* I thought. They wanted fat-free creamer for their coffee and real American ham instead of *jamón serrano* and generally talked loudly and shared food in restaurants in distinctly American ways.

Looking back, I am embarrassed for myself, my little aggressions, my lack of grace.

It was in the middle of that trip that we visited Cambridge: cool and quiet and somehow comforting. Gorgeous college buildings and chapels were softened with mist. We watched punters on the River Cam and had tea in a cozy shop—small tables, ham sandwiches with butter and grated cheese. It was lovely, I was charmed, and I expected Oxford now to be the same.

But Oxford disappointed me with its contrasting noise, dirt, and general commotion.

At the center I found the Bridge of Sighs, the copy of an ornate covered Venetian bridge that looks incredibly romantic in pictures but really just connects one college building to another. Then the Bodleian Library, founded in the 1300s—one of the world's largest—and the round Radcliffe Camera or Rad Cam with its domed top. I eyed the café behind the University Church of St. Mary the Virgin, one of the prettiest spots in town, and made my way down to get a look at the Thames—or the Isis, as they call it here.

On the descent of St. Aldates, I wandered through a bit of meadow by Christ Church Cathedral and began to be enthralled.

I wondered how Jane felt when she arrived here, a child in the midst of the bustle of college life. She came to Oxford when she was seven years old, away from home for the first time to attend boarding school with her sister, Cassandra.[1] She was young to leave home, but the two girls were attached, and as her mother said later, "if Cassandra's head had been going to be cut off Jane would have her's cut off too."[2] Perhaps they traveled with their brother James, who was already enrolled at St. John's College, or perhaps their father took them. Their great witty uncle Theophilus, then ninety,[3] was Master at Balliol College and may have been given the charge of looking after them from time to time. He must have seemed more than ancient to tiny Jane.

Perhaps, I decided, I will come to love Oxford's dirt the way I love Paris's fumes: *I am not without hope.*

⚜

I'm afraid at times I'm morbidly silly. I generally lose the ability to think and act with good sense around guys I could be interested in—just like any good chick-lit heroine, I suppose, but not promising for one who aspires after Austen. My emotions have changed so much in the course of one day. This morning I bumped into a terribly good-looking stranger on the stairs. I was timidly setting off to explore Oxford, in my green T-shirt and matching sort-of-coolish walking shoes and almost knee-length jean skirt with the ruffle (ever so slightly trailer trash but darn cute) when a guy carrying a huge suitcase appeared. I was in his way. I could easily have gotten out of his way if I hadn't been a bit dumbfounded. But there was the jet lag. I wasn't thinking entirely correctly. I took him in immediately—dark wavy hair, green eyes (or were they brown?), great smile, white shirt, bit of a tan—and went on my way with a much lighter heart. I'm afraid I'm looking too much for small, life-changing moments, and when you look for them too closely, you are apt to create them out of nothing at all.

One guy my friends knew of who seemed acceptably interesting, if American, was planning to be in Oxford this week at a program that sounds remarkably similar to the program I am in. He is a friend of Emilie's fiancé, John, and Emilie is a very good friend of my very good friend Jordan (which sounds confusing, but really this connection is simpler than it sounds). Jordan was going to a party at Emilie's, she mentioned that I was getting ready to leave for Oxford, Emilie remembered John's friend…and thus the plotting began.

What we heard from John was that this guy, Frederick Kent is his name, is a lawyer (smart!) and very orthodox. That combination among the single Christian population can be a bit difficult to find. And he is in Oxford, so he must have some sense of adventure, right? And I determined that he would be good-looking, although John gave us frustratingly little information about his appearance.

So as I packed, I wondered exactly what Frederick Kent might be like and just how much potential he might have. When my father dropped me off at the airport at an insanely early hour for my 8:10 a.m. international flight, I wandered through the airport picking out guys— the incredibly good-looking guy I would never have a chance with, the business traveler with a big belly, the Buddhist monk, the devout Muslim with his wife and children, the gawky teenager with his MP3 player—looking at them and thinking, *Ah, Frederick Kent!* and having a little laugh at their expense (or perhaps my own).

Of course, I have decided that the good-looking guy on the stairs must be Frederick, although I suspect this is all very Lydia Bennet of me.

Tonight I walked home with someone entirely different, who is now not a stranger and already feels like he could be much more than a friend. His name is Jack.

I attempted to rule him out. Of course, a single woman who wants to be married has, ironically, no sharper skill than that which rules out potential suitors before fully understanding their character. But I am already afraid that all of my efforts in that vein will be unsuccessful.

Three

Christ Church: Good Company

The more I know of the world,
the more am I convinced that I shall never see a man
whom I can really love. I require so much!

—MARIANNE, *SENSE AND SENSIBILITY*

One day, after I left my job to write full time, I sat in the tiny sunroom of my town house at the café table squinched into the corner by the french doors, reading psalms and thinking about the utter truth of Jesus. In my exhaustion, his character—his complete truth, the kind I have never experienced—was clearer and more important and more true to me than it had ever been. I sat daydreaming in the sun and lost myself in it.

I never entirely recovered from that mono-like virus five years ago. I've been regularly exhausted ever since, something that submits me not only to mood swings but also to dramatic spiritual experiences. I don't know how to explain them, except that in some ways you know things more fully and clearly when you are physically quite at the end of yourself. There are things you miss, I think, when you are able to carry out your daily tasks without ever thinking your psyche might slip through a fissure in the fabric of the universe and you might never recover (though, of course, this is not the best prescription for sanity).

I was weary of the problems I'd had at work, of not being able to get people to listen to the complete story. I had to summarize and synthesize and give them conclusions for which they didn't understand all the background. Then they built on this scant foundation a thought system of their own about my work or the problems we were addressing that was not entirely accurate. Every experience, it seemed, was more complex than anyone else wanted to know. Thus they always had slight half-truths, and I felt scandalized and misrepresented. I began to sense that it is nearly impossible for any of us to *be* completely true when the mass of raw material we are working with—the heart and soul and mind that form our thoughts and desires and words—is so completely faulty to begin with.

I realized then that Jesus knew all the exacts, everything the way it exactly happened, all the intricacies and dependencies and turns of phrase. Also that he is true in a way no one else ever could be—completely and thoroughly, with no shades of doubt, nothing motivated by pride, nothing muddy, everything clear and sound.

This was so important to me as I sat in the sun that I thought about being in the presence of this complete truth and imagined declaring its goodness—his goodness—the way the angels do maybe, proclaiming and honoring him for who he is. I pictured myself going around in front of Jesus everywhere he went in heaven, preceding him, declaring him to be faithful and true and calling the rest of heaven to attention. And I quickly determined that that would get insanely annoying for all of eternity.

Tonight I sat in a row of folding chairs in gorgeous little Christ Church Cathedral, where the air felt dusty and holy, and what hit me with full spiritual force in my exhaustion was the grace and goodness of God—that which I've begun to hope for in the everyday circumstances of my life but not entirely expect. I kept hearing those words in my head, and as I looked up at where the stone arches meet in the ceiling, I could imagine this goodness coming down to me. The Evensong prayers and the hymns and the readings and the gorgeously sung psalms—all of them added up to the message that I am not beyond grace and that perhaps I can hope even now, on this trip, for God's abundant blessings, whatever form those might take.

I don't know what Jane would have made of these terribly serious spiritual musings. She was entrenched in the church because of her father and brothers, but she didn't write anything that would hint at any spiritual angst, any struggle to believe or not believe, or even any deep spiritual emotion. Perhaps her faith was just an accepted part of her life, as steady and unquestioned as the Hampshire seasons. She seems to have judged her own Christian life the way she evaluated those around her—not by what she felt about God, but by how she lived, how she treated others.

Her nephew James Edward wrote about her spiritual reserve, about how she was "more inclined to *think* and *act* than to *talk*"[1] about her faith. Her niece Anna remembered that Aunt Jane would enjoy things to the fullest, but that when she was contemplating serious matters, she would feel them the most deeply as well—"when grave she was *very* grave."[2] So perhaps, at some level, Jane would understand.

What is clear is that Jane operated from a moral foundation. If she knew that others fell short, I believe it was in part because she was aware of her own failings. She crafted stories about lovely, smart, intelligent women—and men—who were blind to their own faults. Pride.

Immaturity. Self-centeredness. These were not small, but impurities of character to be worked out with the help of those who loved you enough to tell you the truth.

For Jane, this working out was genuine faith, this mastery of character as much to be celebrated as the excellent romantic conclusions of her novels. Jane is never heavy handed with this, but I believe the triumph of the books, for her, in the end is not only that the relationships come together but the kind of people who are allowed to come together—two people with characters that have been hammered out a bit, with faults that have been recognized and corrected. They are wise and humble enough to help each other work out their faults and appear guaranteed of some success in that regard.

No one in Jane's stories is spared from this kind of stringent—even in a way harsh—evaluation. *Persuasion*'s Captain Wentworth is not allowed to have been motivated solely by hurt feelings but by "angry pride."[3] He is allowed to be ridiculous, yielding painful consequences to himself and Anne. Emma (in, of course, *Emma*), whom everyone must agree spoke truthfully when she told old Miss Bates that she must limit the number of "very dull"[4] things she said, is not allowed to just laugh it off as a joke. Until Emma recognizes this meanness and, as a result, her propensity to overlook her own faults and need for correction, she cannot be really worthy in Austen's mind. In *Pride and Prejudice*, Darcy as a child "was given good principles, but left to follow them in pride and conceit,"[5] while Anne in *Persuasion* is nearly perfect and is easily guided by Mrs. Russell. She concedes that this is not a moral failing, but her own personality needs a bit of firming up. Meanwhile, Marianne in *Sense and Sensibility* allows her emotions to lead her into questionable situations, readily giving offense and ultimately caring only about her own happiness, while Elinor allows her own very strict moral code to stifle any kind of emotional display. (And although Jane was writing in praise of Elinor's self-control, I cannot read it without feeling like she is too rigid.)

The faults of minor characters are on display as well. Mrs. Bennet is silly throughout *Pride and Prejudice,* while Mr. Bennet does not take enough trouble to discipline his daughters. In *Sense and Sensibility,* Mrs. Jennings is a gossip, and *Emma's* poor Miss Bates cannot stop talking. Mary (Anne's younger sister in *Persuasion*) is never satisfied, determined to be the center of attention, always imagining herself ill (which was one of Jane's favorite failings to mock). And even the nearly perfect Jane Fairfax, also in *Emma,* entered into a questionable engagement without the knowledge of her family.

Those who are more openly in the wrong are not dealt with extensively. In *Sense and Sensibility,* Willoughby deeply regretted losing Marianne, if he had the indignity of not being "forever inconsolable."[6] We know that in *Pride and Prejudice,* Wickham and Lydia quickly fell out of love and seemed destined not to be happy or content. As Lizzy conjectured, "How little of permanent happiness could belong to a couple who were only brought together because their passions were stronger than their virtue."[7] In *Persuasion,* Mr. Elliot, who is only after Anne to gain a standing in the family and prevent another heir being born, is not at all enviable and ends up with the far less appealing Mrs. Clay.

C. S. Lewis said that the world of Austen's novels "is exacting in so far as such obedience is rigidly demanded; neither excuses nor experiments are allowed."[8] At times—especially with Fanny in *Mansfield Park*—she is so particularly moral as to make me a bit weary of it. Yet she is right.

One of her Evening Prayers captures her theology and my own better than I could:

> Look with mercy on the sins we have this day committed and in mercy make us feel them deeply, that our repentance may be sincere, and our resolutions steadfast of endeavouring against the commission of such in future. Teach us to understand the sinfulness of our own hearts, and bring to our knowledge every fault of temper and every evil habit in which we have indulged to the discomfort of our fellow-creatures, and the danger of our own souls. May we now, and on each return of night, consider how the past day has been spent by us, what have been our prevailing thoughts, words and actions during it, and how far we can acquit ourselves of evil. Have we thought irreverently of thee, have we disobeyed thy commandments, have we neglected any known duty, or willingly given pain to any human being? Incline us to ask our hearts these questions oh! God, and save us from deceiving ourselves by pride or vanity.[9]

I suppose it makes me feel that she understands the particulars, the detailed specifics of a situation. She understands the value of a tone of voice or a turn of phrase. She aimed at nothing less than the careful truth.

❧

After Evensong, I began to feel like Anne in *Persuasion* when she says, "My idea of good company, Mr. Elliot, is the company of the clever, well-informed people, who have a great deal of conversation."[10] I was rich with the best kind of company.

I met a couple of guys from D.C. on the way to Christ Church for Evensong. Jack is working on a master's in the classics; Spencer is a writer. We wandered through Oxford after church with their friend Paul, looking for a pub that was still serving food, and we ended up at the Eagle and Child—or the Bird and Baby, as the locals call it. This was where Lewis and Tolkien and the rest of the Inklings took their famous "long liquid lunches" every Tuesday. The place was small and dark, but I loved it for Lewis's sake and felt compelled to drink half a pint in his honor.

Our repartee skittered its way from our religious backgrounds (largely rather conservative, which we all seemed to have moved away from a little) to Christians and politics (Christians in politics—very good; political Christianity—very bad); the shenanigans of various members of Congress; the importance of ending poverty and various other Christian efforts in social justice; and the dangerous cultural trends in American Christianity. The camaraderie was precious. I thought of Jane and all her brothers and the houseful of boys and envied the mélange.

By the end of the conversation, I knew Jack wasn't a typical Christian conservative guy. (Not that there's anything wrong with your typical Christian conservative guy, of course, but I am looking for something slightly different.) He's politically moderate, supports conservation causes, is deeply concerned for the poor, and believes that coming to God is a mysterious process—that God draws us to him and that we freely choose him in a way we can't entirely understand. (Nothing irks me more than guys who will presume to tell you exactly how God works in everyone's life, as though he can be pinpointed and charted out, all the mystery theologized out of him.)

Before the evening was over, I wondered if my preference for the dashing stranger on the stairs had me imitating Marianne's mistakes in some form.

As we walked back to Wycliffe ahead of the others, Jack and I talked about our families. I feel like we are instant friends. He asks if I am a morning person, and I laugh and say, "No. Actually, I can't imagine the possibility of being a morning person in any circumstances ever." And I learn that he is an early riser, almost every day. This little exchange seems to signify something (because the other skill that single women possess is overanalyzing every conversation), our moving from group discussion to near-intimate details.

On the plane to Oxford, when I got up to walk around and prevent said blood-clot danger from flying, I passed a professional-looking guy on the aisle opposite me, two rows up. He was sleeping or watching a movie, and I looked at his screen from two rows back to see what he was watching, but I barely noticed him or his glasses or his neat hair. Now I realize that guy was Jack, in seat 24C. He didn't notice me either, alternately anxious and thrilled, in my pink T-shirt and long jeans and ugly new hiking boots. Just as well. I was having a bad hair day.

⚜

I'm looking for two things in a guy: Someone who loves God with all his heart, with a live and generous faith. And someone who adores me.

And built into those two requirements are all kinds of unspoken assumptions:

He will love learning.

We'll have great, intelligent, funny conversations.

He'll respect me.

He'll be kind.

He'll be basically conservative without being easily annoyed with war protesters.

He'll like to give money away.

He'll be normal—someone I could actually introduce to my non-Christian friends without cringing.

And as Jane would say, he should be good-looking, "which a young man ought likewise to be, if he possibly can."[11] With my apologies to the stellar Christian single guys I've met in the last few years, it's a truth universally acknowledged among single Christian women that single Christian guys beyond a certain age are weird. We used to speculate that it had something to do with the rising sperm count, the lack of sex—that women can handle this, but guys just get weirder and weirder until they are forty-two and completely beyond reach.

And of course, right? The church is a place for the broken. Anyone who doesn't fit in anywhere else is certain of a welcome in the church. If you have trouble putting two sentences together or looking a girl in the eyes, if you are uneducated or only capable of talking to other Christians, or if you're recovering from a cocaine addiction or a messy divorce, come to our church and you'll be welcomed. And that's how it should be.

But it doesn't always make for good dating grounds. (Then there is the other side—the guys who attend church but aren't entirely committed to living their faith, guys who try to explain their theological understanding that sex is acceptable anywhere there is love, whatever else the Bible may say about it.)

It seems as well that there's something about modern evangelical Christianity in America that can encourage a kind of overspiritual weirdness. I went to coffee with one guy, and he prayed loudly for our coffee time together and then asked me questions like, "So what is the Lord teaching you?" which were popular in my high-school youth group but I've since come to loathe, particularly from near strangers.

Modern Christian America is plagued by the sacred/secular dichotomy. If we are talking about the Lord, singing about the Lord, listening to music by other people who love the Lord, wearing T-shirts or bracelets about Jesus, calling a plumber who also loves Jesus, those are good things. Other things, regular, normal things, are suspect. All of which may make for Christians who fear and cannot relate to the world in which they live. The church is full of guys who believe this. I could never go out with them, and they probably think I'm not a very good Christian anyway.

So at thirty-three I sit on the love seat in the sunroom from time to time and pray for an amazing guy—someone normal, someone who loves God with all his heart, someone who will adore me—believing that it's nearly impossible, but that God specializes in those kinds of things when he so chooses.

✣

As someone who's far from a morning person, eating breakfast at 8:00 a.m. in a roomful of strangers is my idea of purgatory. If I could, I wouldn't talk to anyone ever before 10:00 a.m., best friends included. So when I came downstairs wearing my fun pink pleated skirt with the flip-flops that match exactly, I was praying that no one would notice me.

I would have given anything for an invisibility cloak, actually. Most especially, I didn't want to admit the possibility that something romantic could exist here, at least not before I'd had coffee and a decent plate of something substantial.

When I walked into the room, the fire alarm went off. The whole room smelled of toasting bread (alas, no bacon or eggs to be had). Jack was sitting right by the door, looking very good and incredibly awake. He smiled at me and said, "You walk in the room and bells ring. You did good getting up early this morning." I thought to myself, *Crap, he's still here,* and like a schoolgirl I couldn't eat my toast.

Four

Austenian Faith and Love

I feel, alas, that I am dead
In trespasses and sins.

—WILLIAM COWPER, "THE SHINING LIGHT"

I've not always believed in the grace of God. Actually, since I was roughly three, I've believed in the big, eternity-changing, salvation sort of grace. That was when I asked Jesus into my heart, childlike and beautiful, I imagine, during evening prayers in my brother's room. My brother and I knelt on the shag carpet with our hands folded on his seventies comforter. He laughed. At least that's what I tell myself because, actually, I don't remember that anymore. I just used to remember and told myself that version of the story for so many years that now it's fact, even if it didn't actually happen.

As a child in Baptist schools, I prayed that prayer over and over in chapel, at Vacation Bible School during the summer; everyone wanted to know in those days the date and time I prayed the "sinner's prayer." I was never entirely sure which one stuck.

Then in college I wondered if I really believed any of it—God, Jesus, the Bible, the need for salvation. I took two years to feel my way through doubt. I still knew, in some way that I'm not sure I can explain, that God was with me, that he guided me even as I asked questions and investigated what the rest of the world believed. I studied C. S. Lewis's *Mere Christianity* and *Surprised by Joy* and eventually determined that Christianity was true. I felt as if it would take me a lifetime to evaluate all the logical, rational arguments, and I didn't have the brainpower for that or the time, and as much as I could evaluate them, they felt true to me, so I came back. But I came back to a different faith, one that was shaky and easily faltered and could be toppled over into a whirlwind of doubt by the little breath of a series of questions from my brother or a scientific article questioning the existence of Jesus or the occasional realization of the hugeness of the world that did not believe as I did.

But the point is I firmly believed in the love and grace of God. I knew that was one of Christianity's distinctives. I could tell you how to confess your sins and be forgiven "of all unrighteousness," even the things you didn't know you did. But I didn't actually believe in grace for myself, not on a daily basis. And this has been my great struggle: I've often felt like it's impossible to keep up with my confession. I'm simply too wrong in my core. As soon as I confess and receive forgiveness and occasionally feel the depth of that, the cleanness of being right with God, I set off on another pattern of wrong thinking, where I'm the center of my universe, where even when I try to put other people first and love God (and don't always put that much energy into that), I fail miserably and am aware of the fact that seemingly two seconds after I've been irrevocably washed clean, I am dirty again, like filthy rags. And after years of church and faith—being instructed over and over to read my Bible every single day to please God, being taught

implicitly that my spirituality is directly related to the number of services I attend or the number of people I witness to, and being part of
a family that doesn't enjoy or maybe believe in lying about, in taking
three hours by the pool with only a drink and a magazine (we are the
industrious, entrepreneurial type)—I believed in the necessity of earn-
ing the pleasure of God.

I thrived on doing and forgot how to be. When I finally went to
counseling to work through depression, I was in a state in life where I
couldn't even make myself a cup of tea. I watched my roommate make
tea and wondered how she could take the time to do such a thing, to let
the water boil, let the leaves sit, actually slow down enough to drink it.
Everything in my life was about doing. Every minute was scheduled to
take advantage of my limited energy. So I worked until I crashed and
couldn't work any longer. And when I crashed, on my lost days, I could
barely make or eat anything. I couldn't even enjoy watching TV. The days
rushed past as I lay on my couch with pictures going by on the screen
in front of me, too numb and dissociated to be involved in the stories.

Everything was work. Work was my salvation. And not being able
to work made me distraught. It bothered me that I had forgotten
how to relax. I wasn't enjoying life. Part of me must have known that I
couldn't save myself.

⚜

Jack and I got seats together for lectures by the doors that opened to
the back lawn, letting in the gorgeous seventy-something weather.
David Wenham was talking about the Sermon on the Mount, about its
two groups of pronouncements, the first about God's grace and the

second, which can be "profoundly depressing," about God's standards, which are so high that no one can live by them.

I leaned over to tell Jack that I have such a hard time balancing those things, the grace and judgment of God. He said quietly, "Yeah, I've found in my life that the grace has to come first."

◦✢◦

I'm afraid I'll make some people cringe by tying Jane to Christianity in any form. She was not evangelical, though her cousin, clergyman Edward Cooper, was part of the new evangelical movement beginning to sweep the country. Unfortunately, Jane didn't always like his sermons, which she found too full of "Regeneration & Conversion,"[1] and he had a habit of sending "Letters of cruel comfort,"[2] which seems to hint at Mr. Collins. Jane still found a way to admire the young movement, if she found it too "loud and noisy"[3] for her own tastes. She wrote, "I am by no means convinced that we ought not all to be Evangelicals, & am at least persuaded that they who are so from Reason & Feeling, must be happiest & safest."[4] I recognize that Jane's religious experiences must have been far different than mine, but I think in fundamentals of belief we might be much the same.

Jane's books are Christian in that there is a solid Christian moral foundation throughout her writing, but they are not Christian books per se by today's definition. She didn't have to deal with the evangelical culture I was raised in—the one in which Christian things are separate from other normal (or as the church sometimes describes them, "worldly") things.

The Church of England was everywhere in Jane's day, a social norm. Everyone went to church. Everyone believed or feigned belief. Which led to other problems, like rectors who cared more for their incomes than their congregations, and sermons that were perhaps sufficient to entertain or simply endure on a Sunday morning but lacking in spiritual depth. One has only to imagine the torture of being part of Mr. Collins's flock to begin to grasp the weaknesses (evils?) of the church system in Jane's day.

One thing I know Jane and I would agree on is the ridiculousness that the church can bring out, if not encourage, in people. I believe sometimes that as a group, while trying to be good, we do not exert enough effort toward being normal.

Austen understood this. Even in her day, faith was sometimes used as a cloak for ridiculous behavior. She didn't spare anyone like this. For her, it seemed nearly as serious as a moral failing.

❧

There's a lovely spot in the grass by the River Cherwell. If you wander through University Parks heading southeast and continue through a few gates, you will find it. Apparently the Oxford dons used to lay out naked here. Academic dons and nudity don't naturally go together. Today, thankfully, everyone is clothed. It sits in a crook of the small river, so there is water on two sides; there are huge trees and expanses of sun. It's mostly quiet, groups of people talking and solitary people sleeping. A loud crowd of tourists has managed to get a punt stuck in the grass by the bank, and two ten- or eleven-year-old boys have stripped down to their shorts trying to work up the courage to jump in.

Jack and I sat with our quiet conversation in the midst of the summer commotion. I'd never felt so comfortable, so at home, just sitting and talking.

"So what do you think you'll do when you finish grad school?"
I asked.

He hesitated a minute. Everything about him was easy—slow and
calm. "I'm not really sure," he said. "I felt called to do this program,
and I love it, but I'm not sure exactly what I'm going to do when I'm
done. I think it may have something to do with writing."

We talked about my writing and his sisters, and he said something
about his grandmother calling him William. It was the second time I'd
heard him refer to himself as William, and it was like an evil prick in
the middle of all this pleasantness. I had to say what I'd been debating.

"Does...um, does your family call you William?" I willed out
the words.

"Yeah, how did you know that?"

"It's just that you were talking about your family a couple times
and I thought...you said...'William.'" I fumbled.

"Actually, everybody calls me William," he said. "My real name is
Jack William—it's a family name—but everybody calls me William.
When I registered for the school here, I gave them my full name, and
they started sending me stuff as Jack, and I never corrected them. I'm not
sure why. I like it, and I thought it would be kind of fun, and it reminds
me of Lewis, I guess. I don't know."

"Well the weird thing is"—alarms were going off in my head but it
was far too late to stop—"I probably shouldn't tell you this."

"No, go ahead," he said.

"Well, you kind of remind me—I mean you look a little bit like an
old boss I had, and his name was William, and he was sort of, um, horrible. He lied a lot or most of the time. He was really one of the most
horrible people I've ever known. I'm not sure if he knew when he was

telling the truth. I ended up confronting him about some things, and he fired me and lied about the whole thing to make it look like it was my fault. It was more complicated than that, and I didn't handle everything as well as I could have, but it was really horrible."

"Well then, by all means," he said in his gentle southern accent, "call me Jack."

"I've dealt with people like that before," he said. "Actually, there was one situation where I ended up having to confront a guy who was really high up, a guy we were working with—he was a CEO, actually, and the way it happened ended up being in a public forum, but I had to say something because he had to be called on it. I was really worried about it, and I didn't want to come off as arrogant, but it had to be done. Anyway, so I'm not your boss, but I've confronted him." And he laughed—not in a mean laughing-at-me way, but in an it's-all-really-okay way. His saying that made me relieved. Still a tiny bit creeped-out and skeptical, but relieved.

We talked about our common perfectionism, which he seems to be a little further along at mastering, and about my trying to accept and really believe God's grace. He told me about the orphan he loves in South Africa and about how that's when God's grace really broke through for him. A life-changing experience of loving a little girl who didn't want to be loved and didn't deserve love, but Jack loved her anyway, wholeheartedly. At that moment God said to him, "This is how I love you." And that stuck.

We talked about how both of us have a hard time relaxing—the perfectionism thing—and Jack said, "You seem perfectly relaxed now." And I was. And I was insanely, cautiously happy.

Jane makes me think of my own small meannesses. (How much of our lives are spent being mean to one another in small ways?)

I met the dashing stranger from the stairs today. The one I imagined to be Frederick Kent—the friend of a friend's friend's fiancé or something crazy like that. And I greeted him with a series of small meannesses under the guise of politeness. I introduced myself, but with that brief look in my eye and turn of my head and little bit of archness that told him I was already closed to him, that he did not entirely measure up.

I don't know why. Perhaps I was feeling insecure. I probably came across to him as a little arrogant. It was all silly. And to the casual observer it would have seemed just two people meeting each other. But I think he knew I had closed the door on him in that brief period of time.

As it turns out, our theological bents are quite different, and the vibe just wasn't there. To be honest, I am now consumed elsewhere, so maybe I wanted him to not really be a match.

A guy friend told me once that he can tell within thirty seconds if he wants to seriously date a girl. I was deeply offended. I mean, is it really all that superficial? The sound of her voice, he said, and the way she looks—his impression after that thirty seconds is never wrong.

I make those snap judgments myself but admit often to being wrong (Jack, for example) and actually being pleased to be wrong. I love the surprise of finding incredible potential where first I could see none.

And today I seemed determined to find no potential at all where first I imagined loads.

Fickle, fickle woman.

He is not Frederick anyway.

So Frederick Kent is still safe out there somewhere, a bastion of smart, orthodox—and in my imagination very good-looking—potential.

Five

Alarms (Fire and Otherwise)

And now I may dismiss my heroine to the sleepless
couch, which is the true heroine's portion; to a pillow
strewed with thorns and wet with tears. And lucky
may she think herself, if she get another good night's
rest in the course of the next three months.

— NORTHANGER ABBEY

At 11:42 p.m., I still couldn't sleep. My room was Spartan, but not in the quaint old-English-hall way I expected, more in an old-1970s-furniture-and-dirty-orangish-brown-carpet way: institutional cream walls, a dirty blue blanket on a bed that upon close inspection looked like someone had at some point been sick on the middle of the box spring and it was never cleaned.

I've not slept well for so long that I no longer really know how to fall asleep. My exhausted body doesn't actually get sleepy anymore, perhaps because I've had to fight being tired so much to get through the days that my brain's reaction to being worn out is to send adrenaline to stem the tide. So I alternately sink into sleep and jerk awake in what feels like panic. But mostly I lie in bed awake, thinking about things, waiting for sleeping pills to kick in.

The pills themselves are tricky. I don't like how they control me, make me do things I can't do on my own. Tonight I took one, hoping it would be enough to guide me into sleep, but it didn't work; it is a unique kind of torture, being wide-awake, exhausted, and unable to do anything about it.

Another symptom of whatever I have is that I often wake after several hours of sleep, as though my terribly hard-working Dickensian inner self has decided it is time to make the gruel. (But, oh, just the thought of gruel makes me want to throw up even now.)

Sometimes when I have trouble sleeping, I imagine there are demons assigned to me, like Screwtape, poking my soul with a big, mean stick as I begin to drift off. They were active this evening, poking away, keeping me desperately awake.

Not that the things I had to think about were altogether horrible…

⚜

I need a remedial class in dating. Or maybe just in talking to boys.

Wide-awake, exhausted, and nauseous, I watched the sun just beginning to rise. The fire alarm, which seemed to conspire against me, wouldn't stop going off last night, and I eventually grabbed my white hoodie and climbed down the spiral iron fire escape.

The lawn was full, and I lurked in the back of the crowd, in pink-and-green-striped cropped-pant pajamas, trying not to wake up all the way. But when I spotted Jack, Paul, and Spencer, I decided waking up wouldn't be so bad and I joined them.

Jack touched my arm. "Nice stripes," he said, making me want to curl up with him and be cozy.

For an hour it was like college. Paul kept getting calls on his cell phone from friends and kept saying, "I'm in England! Do you know what time it is here?" And as a group we decided that Jack should make reparations for something—the Scandinavians and their pillaging, I think—which was all terribly funny to me because by that point, it was around 1:00 a.m., and I'd taken two sleeping pills.

When they finally let us back in, I was too shy to find Jack and say goodnight. I saw him looking around, maybe for me, and made a subconscious decision to sneak silently back up the stairs.

❧

There are numerous divergences between Jane and me, of course. One of the most significant is that Jane wrote in some way because she was a great conversationalist, full of wit in a day when wit was prized, a sharp observer of society. I write in many ways from weakness rather than strength—because I am at times a poor conversationalist, because there are things I can't sort out when I'm talking to people and have to put in writing to make anyone else see them.

When Jane wrote *Emma,* she told her family that she was creating "a heroine whom no one but myself will much like."[1] I think she was wrong. Fanny Price in *Mansfield Park* is the one I have a hard time loving, with all her timidity and fear. She always seems to feel that she really shouldn't be in the room, that she is unworthy of notice, that she is not worth talking to. Perhaps I don't like Fanny because in some ways I share her weaknesses. I have more humor and strength, yet I manage so often to be queen of the socially awkward moment (a trait that, in some part, I come by honestly, as, at some level at least, it runs in the family, although my brother seems to have entirely escaped it).

I think where I feel closest to Jane is in my singleness—in loving freedom and simultaneously longing for companionship. Jane wanted marriage if she could have a great marriage with real love; she was unwilling to settle for a relationship that was merely a good social move and would give her financial security. She wanted an equal, someone who would be an intellectual rival, who would respect her. She loved her life no doubt. She does not seem to have especially wanted children. But part of her hoped for the unexpectedly, unbelievably good match. Perhaps I am a bit presumptuous, but who could read her books and conclude otherwise?

Jane Austen essentially created the chick-lit genre. We all know the formula—girl meets guy; girl falls in love with guy; guy breaks her heart; girl meets nicer, better-looking guy with more money, and they live happily ever after. Obstacles abound in Austen's stories—lack of money on the part of the otherwise lovely heroine, meddling family members who pull lovers apart because they disapprove of the match— but these things are always overcome by the abundant worth of two good people who truly love each other.

The love stories in Austen's own life echo these themes but without the "happily ever after" ending.

Jane's first love, at twenty, was Tom Lefroy. He was a law student from Ireland, the nephew of her dear friend Anne's husband, and Anne may have introduced them. We know little about the relationship really. Much of what we know of Jane's life is from her letters, but her sister, Cassandra, burned many and mutilated more before passing them on to nieces and nephews late in her life. Perhaps Cassandra cut out the juici-est bits or, as Austen expert Deirdre Le Faye suggests, the parts that could have offended one family member or other.[2] Either way, there are gaps.

Jane and Tom spent some time together during the course of a few weeks, over Christmas and New Year's. He was fairly serious, quiet, and very good—maybe a balance for Jane's energetic humor. They bantered over Henry Fielding's *Tom Jones,* and after a ball, Jane wrote jokingly to Cassandra of "everything most profligate and shocking in the way of dancing and sitting down together."[3] She wrote about how the Lefroy household gives Tom a hard time about the attachment, so that when she pays a visit, he manages to hide. But he would pay her another visit, as was the custom, to thank her for partnering him at the ball, and the only fault she could really find with him was that his morning coat was "a great deal too light."[4]

There is much debate these days about just how in love Jane was with Tom and how much this relationship influenced her writing. Some say it was just a flirtation—clearly, in Jane's letters, she is being sarcastic, they say. To me she writes as if there is some depth to her feel-ings in spite of trying to laugh them off. "I rather expect to receive an offer from my friend in the course of the evening," she writes of their last meeting. "I shall refuse him, however, unless he promises to give away his white Coat."[5] She sounds a little bit like my friends and I as well, telling stories of a romance that fell into the middle of a life that was largely without romantic interest, making much of a little thing. Yet it's easy to imagine her being teasing and sharp with Tom.

Tom was from a good family but not wealthy. His father had been in the army. He was the oldest son, but it was a large family, eleven chil-dren with five daughters ahead of Tom, and he was made to feel that the future of the family was on his shoulders.[6] He was expected to do well, to do much. Though the attachment seems to have been mutual, Anne and her husband stepped in and quickly sent Tom home. The family history is that Anne Lefroy was forever frustrated with Tom over this, his leading Jane on when he knew there was no chance he could propose.[7]

Tom eventually married someone with an appropriately large fortune, had seven children, and went on to become Lord Chief Justice of Ireland.[8] He was no Darcy—not heir to great estates or wealth—but clearly his family had expectations Jane did not meet. If Jane wrote about family interference, she'd learned it firsthand. Tom may have adored her and she him, but she hadn't enough money to qualify. Most likely Jane never saw him again.

When it ended, Jane wrote to Cassandra: "At length the day is come on which I am to flirt my last with Tom Lefroy, & when you receive this it will be over—My tears flow as I write, at the melancholy idea."[9] She was joking, of course. How deeply she felt the joke we will never really know. But her heart had been engaged for likely the first time.

No doubt this relationship and her repartee with Tom fueled her writing. Mine will be fueled in part by things like climbing quietly back up the stairs when I really just wanted to say goodnight.

⁂

The course of true love never did run smooth and all that. Yet should it be abandoned at that first halting difficulty? At this point in my life I am willing to err on the side of giving it more opportunity to prove itself true.

Jack and I wandered through Oxford on an absolutely perfect seventy-something afternoon like tourists, taking pictures. We made our way slowly through town—first Trinity College, then the Bodleian, and then our real destination of Magdalen College, where Lewis taught, which the guidebook calls "perhaps the most typical and beautiful Oxford college."[10]

Magdalen is gorgeous and immediately became one of my favorite places. It took us awhile to figure out the lay of the land, and we wandered into one of the fifteenth-century cloisters, with detailed fretwork in the archways, wonderful gargoyles, and a view of the bell tower just beyond where the college choir sings every May Day morning. Jack was taking my picture in one of the arches when a young guy, a tourist, offered to take our picture together and pronounced it "beautiful." So there it was—the first somewhat awkward record of a friendship.

We wandered out from the cloisters into an expanse of open sun and manicured lawn, the imposing New Building—"new" being relative, as it was new in 1733—directly ahead and on the right, a ways off, a lovely flower garden bordering Holywell Mill Stream and a little bridge over the river leading to Addison's Walk. The walk is about a mile round, often by the river, through a bit of wilderness where they sometimes graze the college flock of deer. It's here where C. S. Lewis, J. R. R. Tolkien, and Hugo Dyson walked, talking about faith, just before Lewis converted.

Jack and I hung out on the bridge for a while, looking at the flowers, watching the water birds. Jack took a picture of me on the bridge; I generally hate pictures. They often manage to catch my weak chin at just the wrong angle so it looks like I have no chin at all. But my new theory is that one shouldn't strive to be beautiful. It's something to just be good-looking enough, and if you really smile in pictures and forget to worry about what you look like, they turn out surprisingly well.

And maybe that state of mind worked. This one caught the infectious grin that was becoming my natural state.

We started talking as we walked into town, and for the nearly four hours we were together we just talked. I'm not sure that these kinds of conversations can be accurately re-created (or perhaps that I'm capable of re-creating them). They are about small things that take on great importance because all of a sudden this other person has become the most important person in your life, at least for today, probably for tomorrow, and—if you're both lucky—maybe for a long time after that.

Over Frappuccinos, Jack said somewhat awkwardly, "Since you write about singles stuff, I should tell you, I...um...I actually just started kind of seeing someone in North Carolina. Not that I'm not enjoying hanging out, but I wasn't expecting to meet someone. You know, this other thing just started, and I...I wasn't looking for anything."

"Oh—well, I really appreciate your telling me," I said, mustering confidence and calmness, like I had been expecting this. "That means a lot." I then proceeded to say something awkward, about a friend who had flown up from Atlanta to take me to dinner, as if to prove that I had relationship ties in the South as well. Inside I smarted. *What was I thinking? Argh. And so what if there's a girl in North Carolina? I'm here now and you like me, right?*

Jack said he and this girl had just started going out; their relationship wasn't really defined yet; he didn't know what was going to happen with it. But he wanted me to know. In some way that seemed very honorable, and somehow strange, and ultimately irrelevant. Serious enough to tell me and not serious enough to actually *be* anything. I was rattled and determined to see this as somehow chivalric.

We moved on to things that can take months to get to in the course of everyday dating—his uncertainty about marriage and kids, my eagerness for them downplayed—trying to display it in the best possible light.

Then we wandered through Christ Church Meadow for a while, all the way down the broad, gravel walking path to the River Isis and back, talking about all the stuff of life we have in common. He asked me what I wanted or enjoyed. I talked about renting a villa in Italy and inviting my friends, wanting to be fluent in Spanish and French and Italian, wanting to learn Greek and Hebrew and understand the cultural and historical setting of Jesus and write about those things, wanting to figure out how to really help the poor.

He understood everything.

In so many places our desires and goals seemed the same, or at least coming from such a similar place.

"There are so many things I want to do. I'm afraid life won't be long enough," I said.

Jack replied slowly, "Well, you know, you don't have to do everything now."

⚜

I seemed to be perfecting a certain *eau de travel* and realized that the smells on this trip were all wrong. When I first opened my suitcase, I found a printed note saying that the TSA had inspected my bag and everything might not have been put back in the right place. It smelled horrible, like one of the paint compounds from my dad's hobby room where he works on his airplane models. I thought, *Great, they've used some kind of chemical in my bag to detect traces of bombs, and now all my clothes smell.* But it turned out to be my Professional Firma Nail Extra Strength Base and Top Coat (a manicure kit is a must), which had leaked into its small plastic zippered bag and somehow managed to infect all of my clothes. Ugh.

My underwear were in an old ditty bag from my backpacking days, which had infused them with the tang of cheap plastic. In a moment of inspiration, wondering at my own excessive preparedness, I pulled out dryer sheets from my laundry supplies and stuffed one in there and spread a few throughout my clothes. But now I began to sicken at the spicy, overwrought smell, which still didn't cover the bad rubber/chemical tinge my clothes had acquired.

And then there were my lovely new green slip-on tennis shoes. I knew they might be a problem because they made my feet unusually hot, and sure enough, a foul case of foot odor was brewing. I'm not typically the foot-odor type. Seriously. But this wafted up from the region of my ankles and surrounded me in a Pigpen-like cloud.

Even my lips became less than lovely. The special ChapStick I had bought for the trip smelled pungent like medicine, and my cheap trashy-sparkly lip gloss hinted of chemicals rather than berries.

So my stinky feet and I put on our flip-flops and sweatpants and headed out on the lawn to smoke Cubans with Jack and Paul.

We sat in the wet grass, the evening glowing with the luminescent, late blue hour, the hour of dusk that many believe to be holy. (I am among them.) Eventually, we were lit by nothing but lights from the windows.

Paul, raised in a good, strict Assemblies of God home, chose to abstain. "Smoke a cigar and go to hell? No, I don't think so." He laughed.

We talked about grace and alcohol, about how Jesus might have acted at a party, about Paul's brother, who had been an alcoholic and then was miraculously cured.

I told Paul and Jack about only recently discovering that I grew up with a view of the world where there were good people (Christians) and bad people (everyone else) and how I'd finally realized that I had been looking down at the world all these years and knew that we are all loved the same and all flawed the same—all of us equal before God. That God could be just as present at a party where guys were smoking joints on the back porch as he was at my Bible study—present in a different way, but still present and reaching.

When you see the world this way, any place can be holy.

All of that talk of some other girl in North Carolina has been forgotten.

I don't know exactly what it means to fall in love or what I think about that, so I'm not sure how to talk about what has been happening between Jack and me. Fundamentally, I believe that *love* is a verb, that it is doing things you may not feel like doing and giving and listening and generally putting someone else in front of yourself. Perhaps it's not possible to make that kind of commitment for a lifetime without an initial rush of emotion. Sunday night after we met, when we went to Evensong and to the pub and walked home talking about our families and mornings and evenings, I knew this had potential. Last night I thought it could be serious. And tonight I know—well, I'm not sure exactly what—perhaps that he is The Guy I Never Thought I Would Meet.

My perception of time has changed. There are so many significant moments, so many in each day that the days feel stretched into weeks, and I don't doubt that by the end of the week, I will feel like we've known each other for six months. The contrast between days in Oxford and days at home—which can pass distractedly with a couple loads of laundry, a movie, and a Target run—makes me feel the malleable subjectivity of time.

Unlike other relationships I've had, my love for Jack seems to have depth and stability, to be founded on mutual faith and genuine respect, honest intellectual conversations, strong doses of humor and comfort. So our attraction has something solid on which to play. It's all rather Austenian.

In some ways, this Big Thing is a combination of hundreds of tiny important things. If alone they are small, together they are undeniable, pointing to something true and sound, of incredible value—pointing to us.

At least, it seems that way to me.

❧

I am, actually, afraid that people will look back on my own scant love life someday and assume that nothing ever happened, that my heart was never touched. And I wonder if my life will turn out more like Jane's life or like the heroines' lives in her books.

I sat looking out the patisserie window, streaming and sniffling, trying to eat a chocolate croissant.

I woke to the darkness of 3:30 a.m., after just three and a half hours of sleep. I lay awake through the gradual graying of the sky coming in through my open window, listening to the birds, turning things over and back again in my mind—bits of conversations, the way Jack and I fit, the perfection of it all. I was in awe at the certainty of it, having never felt so strongly about someone in so short a period of time, for reasons that seemed incredibly sound. I wanted to go to breakfast alone, to not have to exert the energy to talk to strangers—to talk to anyone.

By 5:15, my body was desperate to be asleep again. This is the hardest kind of sleep to fight—everything heavy and weighty; I am held to the pillow as if by some kind of great force. But I fought it anyway because I didn't want to sleep through things. I sat up and stretched on my bed in the soft dawn, trying to make sense of the world without success.

Jack caught me on my way out, just when I was hoping I wouldn't see him. He must have been watching for me and was eager to talk about some passages he was reading to follow up on our conversation of the night before. I told him with some regret that I needed to be alone. Part of me wants him to just disappear. I am too tired to be in love.

The patisserie is on a small, quiet street full of restaurants, a pub, a sandwich place, and a florist. There is a full window along the front, with a bar running across it. By the time I sat down with everything—cranberry juice, cappuccino, water, and two chocolate croissants—I began to sense just how much trouble I was in. I was devastatingly tired.

I started to cry and couldn't stop—not a loud, shaking, full-on cry, but a quiet stream, as though God had turned the faucet on low. I was afraid of the surety I felt. I thought I never could have imagined Jack so well. I was overwhelmingly grateful. And I knew I would never be able to sort out my emotions through so much exhaustion. So I decided to let myself cry.

Jane may have loved, but she never married. You could say her love life was a comedy of errors if it wasn't also a bit tragic and somewhat scant. In addition to her letters, we have recollections from various family members—her brother Henry, her nephew James, and nieces Anna and Caroline. They also recorded some of her sister, Cassandra's, memories of Jane, which she never wrote down. Altogether not a clear picture, but enough to piece together several relationships that did not work out.

After Tom Lefroy, her friend Anne's dashing nephew, there was Revd. Samuel Blackall,[11] a somewhat ridiculous clergyman Anne invited to visit and hoped Jane would form an attachment with (perhaps a model for Mr. Collins?). Jane could never see him as anything but laughable—"a peice of Perfection, noisy Perfection himself."[12] Blackall got the hint and did not return to Hampshire, though he would have liked to. Jane wrote to Cassandra, "It is therefore most probable that our indifference will soon be mutual, unless his regard, which appeared to spring from knowing nothing of me at first, is best supported by never seeing me."[13]

The next significant relationship was with a man from the neighborhood, Harris Bigg-Wither,[14] the younger brother of Jane's dear friends. Jane was just about to turn twenty-seven, old enough to no longer expect to marry—Anne's age when *Persuasion* begins. Harris was an excellent and prudent match, set to inherit the large Manydown estate—ironically the place where Jane had danced so happily with Tom Lefroy—though he was awkward and shy and stammered.[15] He proposed one night when Jane and her sister, Cassandra, were visiting. She accepted him, then apparently stayed up much of the night reconsidering, withdrew her consent in the morning, and hastily left the house in disgrace. It seems there was money but no love, and for Jane that would never do. The match would have given her "all worldly advantages."[16] Almost any other woman of Jane's age in this situation would have accepted Harris and hoped to learn to love him, or determined to live without love, but Jane could not.

There are rumors of another, of a man Jane and her sister met when vacationing at the seaside in Devon. He expressed some interest, which Jane apparently returned. But though the sisters expected to hear from him, they only received news of his death. The details of this relationship are especially murky. They met one summer, and he asked to see the girls the next summer, which doesn't sound terribly promising. But it seems that Cassandra thought he would pursue Jane and expected him to be successful. Either way, what we do know is that he died unexpectedly, and the girls never saw him again.[17]

There were others—occasionally rich, sometimes flirtatious, one who may have proposed and another who thought about proposing and never did—but there was no one else Austen seemed to have been genuinely interested in.

Austen's nephew made light of these romantic experiences, praising Jane's imagination and musing that her heart had never been touched, and her brother Henry doesn't mention them at all. But no woman who has fallen in love at twenty or contemplated marrying a man she didn't truly love can believe that Jane was emotionally removed from these situations. They may seem small and unimportant, but no doubt her heart was involved to some degree or another.

I started dating at sixteen: Miller, a great-looking guy from my small, overwhelmingly Baptist school. Blond hair, blue eyes, football player. Nice. He played King David in one of our high-school dramas when he was a sophomore and I was in ninth grade, and I fell in love with him in the "man after God's own heart" role. That year I asked him to be my escort for homecoming. It wasn't a dance—we never had any dancing because according to Baptist doctrine dancing is sin—but a ceremony between basketball games (our homecoming was in January) where all the class representatives walked out, for some reason in this case in matching long skirts carrying fake flowers. I got the biggest zit I've ever gotten right on the top of my nose, and he walked with me across the gym floor, and I didn't know what to say to him. Two years later we were dating. He gave me such sickly sweet gifts—a necklace that said "Someone Special" (which I still have), a big white teddy bear carrying a red heart—that I had to call it off.

Ten years later, after several college near misses, after dating the wonderful preacher's boy from our church whom I had little in common with, I dated Brian. From time to time, I thought I would marry him. We dated a year, and then he broke my heart and continued to flirt with me for a year at work. Devastated me would get my hopes up and have them crushed, get my hopes up and have them crushed again, over and over. Finally he moved to North Carolina. We sat outside at Anita's, the cheap Mexican place right by Route 50, before he left. He cried and held my hands as we talked about saying good-bye. And then he left. And finally I moved on.

Now, after a years-long drought, here I am in England, unable to finish my chocolate croissant.

Simple Conversation

*Mary wished to say something
very sensible, but knew not how.*

—*Pride and Prejudice*

At some point, every relationship becomes quotidian. It becomes about the daily things, the mundane and menial things; sometimes those menial things, completely unimportant to others, have the greatest effect on our happiness. Especially at the beginning of a relationship, I think, we as women sift through this daily stew of conversations and mannerisms like tea leaves, looking for signs of future happiness or disappointment, love or loneliness. It is a skill we acquire in junior high and never lose.

I made the decision to talk to Jack, looking for reassurance. I wanted him to know that I was a mess, temporarily, but I was really okay. I sensed that this was perhaps a mistake, but when I am overwhelmingly tired and emotional and begin to feel that something *must* be done, I am compelled to do it.

I waited on the lawn for him to finish breakfast, my eyes still streaming as I sat on a green plastic chair under a tent and tried not to make eye contact with anyone, shakily drinking my cappuccino. Who knows what I looked like; I felt like I never entirely made it into the real world that morning and couldn't help it.

And who knew what Jack was expecting—certainly not me in my fragile state. I told him that the last couple days had been intense, that I had not been sleeping well, that I was feeling emotional and couldn't process things, that if I lay low today that was why.

"Wow," he said. "I don't really know what to do with that."

I laughed through tears. "Yeah. Most guys don't."

As I began to sense that assurance would not come, he said, "I'm glad you said something because I've been thinking, we need to make sure we're getting everything we're supposed to out of this week, meeting everyone we're supposed to meet. It probably would be good if we didn't spend so much time together."

I felt the full weight of the blow. I had given him reason to think I am a bit crazy. And I am. Of course, I agreed. It would be good to not spend so much time together, take a step back, hang out with other people. But inside I thought, *Buck up, little camper.*

I imagined him discussing this with the other guys, all of them wondering at my instability, and longed to hang out with a girlfriend who could help me put it all right again, at least in my head.

I got a sandwich from down the street and ate lunch by myself on the library steps. I made plans to go to dinner with someone else and was generally awkward all afternoon, thinking, *Perhaps this Big Thing will end up being nothing after all. I will go back to my quiet little life.*

One topic every Austen biographer must address is her quiet, seemingly eventless life, which is how Jane's brother described it in his first biographical sketch and how her nephew characterized her. To her brother Henry, she was the homebound sister, and to nephew James, she was dear Aunt Jane—funny, charming, full of life, and no doubt unquestionably talented. But what really happened in her life? And so the biographers dig and find love, heartbreak, family conflict, the loss of her beloved childhood home, periods of great financial insecurity, dear friends, and tragic deaths. "Her life was not without event," they say.

And I think, *Of course.* How many of our lives would people judge as entirely unremarkable—lives in which perhaps love fails, careers are made or broken, deep friendships and family relationships endure, tragedy is in some form or other inescapable, and the future is murky. These are our realities, and that's where Jane specialized: the drama of ordinary life, lives not inflated beyond recognition and not with unbelievable goodness or incredible tragedy. Just mothers and fathers, sisters, friends. Pesky neighbors and rich neighbors and neighbors who like you but still want to get the better of you. At times, ridiculous clergy. Good-looking, weak-charactered men; good-hearted plain men; unbelievably rich men with character faults all their own. Fabulous romantic beginnings that may end up being nothing after all. Everyone's foibles on display, with a bit of grace for nearly every character.

Somehow I ended up in Jack's group for dinner, sitting next to him, and by the end of the meal, after trading a few small sharpish sorts of comments and a lot of laughter, we were friends once again.

Several of us decided on a whim to go to a Baroque candlelight concert at Exeter College Chapel after dinner. On the sides, from about eight feet up, the walls are gorgeous stained glass, images of biblical stories clear to the top. It reminds me of a heavier version of Paris's glorious, tiny Sainte-Chapelle. We sat listening to the cello and harpsichord, the readings from Shakespeare ("Let me not to the marriage of true minds admit impediments...") and Queen Elizabeth ("I have the heart and stomach of a king..."), trying to sort out which stories were which in the glass. It was lovely.

We got ice cream and stood talking on the bridge over the Isis, and I was afraid I might pass out from exhaustion.

Walking back, I said to Jack, "I'm not sure exactly what I said to you this morning, and I'm even less sure about what you heard." He laughed a little. I was determined: "I just want to make sure I didn't communicate that I'm not interested, because I am."

"I appreciate that," he said. And quietly, "No, I just heard you say that, you know, you were feeling emotional and needed some space."

"Good."

"You know, it's like I said," he continued. "This other thing just started, and I didn't expect to meet someone—especially someone I had so much in common with. I'm sure you weren't expecting to meet anyone either."

"No, I wasn't." I lied through my teeth. What's a girl to do?

Back in the lobby, I practically whispered, "So then, I'm like, are we just hanging out or what? And I know I don't need an answer to that question now."

But Jack answered me anyway. "Yeah, we should view it that way and not feel like we need to sit together in lectures all the time or spend all our time together. You know, I just don't know what God's going to do with this."

I thought, *Yes, in some sense that's true, but doesn't it just come down to what Jack wants? Isn't that how God generally directs in these situations? And how could he want the girl in North Carolina instead of me?*

We sat in the common room with Spencer, laughing until about midnight when I went upstairs. Jack smiled at me when he said goodnight, said it was a nice night and he'd had a good time. It was.

Officially, nothing is going on between Jack and me.

Strangely, that feels remarkably good. And still, I am treasuring these days and these simple conversations.

◦⁂◦

Perhaps I should make an effort not to see everyone else's faults so clearly. I love everyone close to me, and as for everyone else, I am naturally inclined rather not to like people, to just be content with my small group of lovely friends.

All of my wash has gone slightly gray, and I'm afraid that I dropped underwear on the lawn and they will be pinned to the notice board in the morning. We were sitting outside for a couple of hours with a group, talking, waiting for the washing machines. I just wanted Jack to myself, but he was so incredibly happy to be with people.

I think he is predisposed to love everyone he meets, to want to know everyone. He is like Bingley and Jane; he looks around and sees only good. I look around and catch ridiculous tendencies and sometimes am just too tired to put forth the effort not to be bored. I have been considering the character flaw to be his, but I suppose it must be my own.

Biographers sometimes wrestle with Austen's complex character—the good Christian girl with the biting wit, with the ability to see and desire to expose the laughable and ludicrous. Most of the things that surprise them are in her letters to her sister, Cassandra, where (and perhaps the only place) she could freely say whatever she wanted.

Maybe this doesn't surprise me because of my own experiences. My closest friends and I, if unquestionably faithful, are not overwhelmingly or unnaturally good—at least not blandly so. Our conversations range from incisive devotional thoughts to solving poverty to the creepy, ogling married guys buying us drinks downtown. It's no surprise to me that Jane's life encompassed both as well—that she had a capacity for devotion as well as an ability to wryly, if at times harshly, engage the world around her.

She was not quick to love people outside her little circle, and that is a failing with which I can easily sympathize—one that, at some level, surely comes from some kind of insecurity. Oh well. It is much more fun to be annoyed with Jack and his determinedly loving everyone than to ponder my own failings.

⋙⋘

There is a woman who walks St. Aldates and the Folly Bridge at night. Seeing her for the second time, I notice how she mumbles and shuffles, rather well dressed for someone who may be crazy, in a matching long skirt and blouse. She works her hands together and looks at the ground and sort of hunches along. I wanted to know what she talks about and if anyone ever listens to her. I wondered, does she have children, and do they know this is how she spends her evenings? Does she have friends?

Our loud group passed her on the way to the Head of the River pub, after our farewell banquet in Wadham College's four-hundred-year-old dining hall. I was in my favorite red Ann Taylor dress that's sleeveless, cut in to bare all of my shoulders, and falls to midcalf, grazing my minimal curves. I got to see that instant look of the best kind of surprise on Jack's face when I walked out on the lawn.

As we walked to dinner—together in the crowd, as always—he said, "I was thinking, we should get pictures together." So there we are, looking couplish, standing on the manicured lawn of the Wadham quad.

I laughed that night like I hadn't laughed in ages, healing laughter. Lily got a Long Island Iced Tea, and they doubled the alcohol by mistake. The rest of us didn't need much motivation; our hearts were limber.

I had spent an hour that afternoon back at the spot by the river, lying in the sun. I drifted in and out of sleep, afraid that I could actually sleep soundly there in the middle of the afternoon and not wake up until the sky was gray and I had missed everything. When you live like this—awake and exhausted almost all the time—you can never tell when sleep will come. You sort of have to obey it whenever it wants to make an appearance, but here I was denying it again. I paid for it later, as the unending laughter had me fighting off dry heaves, which have been making regular appearances every morning.

In England they shut down all the pubs at 11:00 p.m. for some reason, as the result of some horrible law (which I understand they have now changed). When they kicked us out, we split up into smaller groups and wandered slowly back through town. We passed Christ Church again, curtains blowing by an open pane, passed lines of people on Cornmarket waiting for the midnight release of the new Harry Potter book, walked up St. Giles, always the quiet heaviness of the Oxford college buildings playing the counterpoint to our lightness. I walked next to Jack, close and connected somehow in spite of the fact that we did not touch—him with his arms crossed, me occasionally letting my hand hang free by my side. We didn't stop laughing, nor did I try to conceal the occasional dry heaves, until we got back to Wycliffe, and then with the sad realization that this was the end of our party.

Everyone leaves tomorrow. Spencer goes back home to a job he wants to leave, Paul to a busy practice. Lily is going on a missions trip to work with disadvantaged youth in London, Jack to Jordan for research for his master's degree, me to a quiet Benedictine monastery in Hampshire, near Jane's home.

I have no idea what to expect, but I long for the peace of the monks.

Seven

Alton Abbey: Incense and Blooms

A lady's imagination is very rapid;
it jumps from admiration to love, from love
to matrimony in a moment.

—MR. DARCY, *PRIDE AND PREJUDICE*

I felt soft and light as I left Oxford the next afternoon. The whole world was beautiful, or my mind was just in a state to see beauty everywhere, like poet James Wright said: "If I stepped out of my body I would break into blossom."[1] The sun shone on the trees and on the vines that grew over the train tracks, and four trains—first to Reading, then to Ash, Aldershot, and Alton—took me from commercial Oxford into the hills and wheat fields of the green countryside. I was thrilled to be on my own—gloriously alone—me and my sixty pounds of luggage and my rail pass.

My mind was full of goodness, of a tremendous confidence I cannot articulate—of Jack's regard, of my respect for him and his worthiness of it. I am sure I love him, though I'm afraid of using that word. I've never felt so sure of anything in my life. I'm not so silly as to begin to speculate about exactly what it will mean, though I wonder what form it will take, how long it will take to meander through casual dinners to beach trips with friends and holidays with family, to its perhaps inevitable conclusion.

When you deal with regular insomnia and fatigue, you reach a point at which your sleeping and waking selves are very much alike. The main differences being that when you are "sleeping" your eyes are closed, and when you are "awake" you are ever so slightly more coherent. Such was my state of being this morning. On these days, I have trouble eating anything, and a flight of stairs can seem insurmountable. I find myself in a kind of stupor where time acts out of character—I may be doing nothing but daydreaming or looking at a book without actually comprehending words or shutting my eyes to pretend to rest, and hours pass in the space of what should be fifteen minutes.

❧

Jack's small words had been incredibly kind that last day in Oxford. He wished me good morning—such a small thing—more than once, with so much energy and attention, with such a kind look that if you saw it, you would forgive me for feeling it to be significant. There's a way couples talk to each other, and Jack started talking to me, looking at me, that particular way. To be so far at the end of myself and to be met with this affection made me feel warm and loved.

But I knew (and felt rather spitefully) the insecurity of all the looks and all the *good morning*s. There was still the girl in North Carolina. We were still officially just hanging out, whatever that meant. I knew there was nothing solid to back up all of these small goodnesses, and so I did not always reply in kind.

I'm afraid at times I gave him little meannesses in return.

Generally though, I was guarded, attempting to be stalwart Elinor and not betray the depth of my feelings. We sat drinking tea at a patisserie on our way downtown to meet Spencer for lunch, and I told Jack that he and my roommate would probably have a lot in common in a teasing way that could have implied I'd like to set them up. I was almost daring him to say something, to tell me with words what his actions and looks had been saying all week. He was not entirely functional this morning either, but he didn't slip. He said nothing substantial, nothing to give me false hope.

When we were alone close to St. Mary's, he looked at me and said, "Well, it's been great hanging out with you this week."

So that's it, I thought and then said, with far less warmth than I felt and with a chilled heart, "Yeah, it's been great."

When it came time to actually say good-bye, I left them both on a little overgrown road outside of Oxford, in front of the place they would stay overnight tonight before heading out tomorrow. Spencer kissed me warmly on the cheek and gave me a close hug, talking about how wonderful the week was and how we would definitely have to get together when we got home and how I must meet his fiancée. And then he made himself scarce—getting his luggage out of the cab, I think—and I turned and saw Jack leaning over to kiss me on the cheek.

His bending down to meet me was so rare for this week of falling into something like love that it startled me, in the best way. We barely touched all week, Jack and I, but I remember him putting his hand on my back once, making sure I made it across the street, and our legs touched briefly by accident as we sat listening to Baroque music in the corner of candlelit Exeter College Chapel. But that's it.

So for a moment I felt lost in him, in this simple closeness. I threw my arms around him and buried my face in his neck and kissed him just there, wherever my lips happened to be, awkwardly and spontaneously. My heart danced. My tongue was stilted as usual. I couldn't say even half of what I'd said to Spencer in genuine friendship. Jack didn't do much better. He told me we'd get together when I got home and, as I went away, called out something about not working too hard.

There is one particular scene in the BBC version of *Pride and Prejudice* that may be my favorite. I sometimes have to go back and watch it again, even though nothing happens. Elizabeth is at the piano, helping Georgiana, and Darcy—Colin Firth—just gazes at Elizabeth for a moment, with complete adoration. That's it. One moment, the best possible look on his face. I never thought to be looked at that way. I mean, it's a movie after all and a Jane Austen movie at that. How many guys just sit back and give a girl adoring glances like they are wholly entranced—in a way that's more than just wanting to get her into bed?

But when I left, Jack had the best look in his eyes—like he couldn't smile enough so it was coming out everywhere else. It was more than happiness. For those few moments I was adored, and the feeling was so strong as to be tangible, sending me off with the confidence of something I didn't dare put into words.

And then I was alone with this great goodness, this thing that no one around me would ever guess.

⚜

My welcome to Hampshire was soft and quiet—the dusky air, the green trees overarching the stone buildings of Alton Abbey. There are many kinds of love, and what I needed most now was not captivating and energetic romance, but the quiet kindness of hospitality, which I found here in abundance. (It was just as well, this being my state of mind, that I was staying in a monastery, where they were well-equipped to lavish me with the one and could never begin to approach the other.) My elation and certainty waned; my exhaustion began to take over.

My cab pulled into the parking lot at exactly the wrong time, around ten to eight. ("Right. Jane Austen. So you're American, yeah? Always the Americans and the Japanese too, tourists, coming to see Jane Austen stuff. Don't understand it myself.") The brothers were in the chapel praying or meeting. Dom Nicholas, the guest master, heard my car and came to meet me, slightly bent, feet moving fast beneath his ankle-length black robes.

"Mrs. Smith," he called me. I guessed he might be somewhere between sixty and seventy, though which end of that I am not sure, with whitening hair and softening skin. He was about six feet tall, on the thin side, and carried my terribly heavy bag up the stairs before treating me to a half-whispered tour with his Irish lilt.

My room spoke of solace: terribly clean, a worn parquet floor, two twin beds with duvets, a large window overlooking the wide lawn and rose garden. The monks' quarters were down the hall, behind a closed door.

The abbey itself is big and meandering. It's what you would expect: simple but lovely, with a beauty in spite of its more functional practicality. It must feel small to the six or eight men who live here—the abbot has been here forty years. Still, it took me awhile to get my bearings. The hall and wide stairway outside my room have windows looking out on a central stone courtyard, with benches and water plants and a fountain. Downstairs there's a huge great room, with five or six couches, bookshelves, and old-fashioned bay windows looking onto the garden. Next door in the dining room, our meals would be taken in silence. Around the corner and down a hall is the entrance to the church, which forms one side of the seemingly square structure.

I feared that I would inevitably do something to offend the monks. Their goal is to welcome all as they would welcome Christ, and I knew I was welcome, yet they live by a strict code with which I'm largely unfamiliar (aside from my reading Kathleen Norris's *The Cloister Walk*). I wonder how often they experience a tension between their Benedictine way and their ignorant guests.

Dom Nicholas showed me the bathroom down the hall, still in an earnest whisper, charging me to remember to leave the rubber shower mat out to dry on the edge of the tub, rather than on the heater where it would melt. He graciously brought me three towels since my own was dirty and asked several times to make sure I had soap.

I joined them in the church for night prayer. These are sort of formal dances of prayers—psalms read responsively, almost chanted, in a strong monotone, a few simple melodies with no accompaniment. I was raised not with this but with the most casual kind of verbal freestyle with God, which I still use. I've grown to love the more formal prayers because they often remind me of things I cannot remember myself, a strong rope of what perhaps in some cases may become rote, but to me helps bind my heart and my faith when I don't have words of my own, when I can't entirely remember exactly what I believe. I feel tied by them to generations of Christians who prayed the same words, thought the same things, had the same doubts.

Three English women were also staying at the monastery on retreat, so the four of us sat in the first row. The prayers brought me a sense of great peace and comfort, and I felt like I had met with not only clean towels and a shower mat that must not melt, but with the hospitality of God. I was welcome here. They welcomed me as Jesus would welcome me, and Jesus would never turn me away. We sang a hymn as the day closed and the sky darkened, and then the monks filed out, raising the hoods of their robes. They would not talk to anyone until morning.

The other guests—Susan, Lane, and Catherine—invited me to join them for a cup of tea, but what I wanted more than anything else was to be alone. So at the end of the day I sat in the narrow ceramic tub, full of the sense of peace, feeling as though I had entered the silence, though sure to put the shower mat back in its proper place.

⁕

I struggle to know what it means to trust God—the God who gives both beautiful and terrible things. The church that morning was filled with the musky sweetness of incense, thick fragrance pouring out of the abbot's swinging censer, overwhelming the small space. I thought I would throw up, then decided instead to try to drink in the scents, like the grace I desperately needed. I often choke on the grace of God.

The day became a lost one, a day to recover. I needed rest. I prayed that God would heal my body and comfort my heart.

I had gone to church without showering, in my T-shirt and jeans and hiking boots, thinking it would be just the four of us like last night. Of course, it wasn't—there was a full congregation in their Sunday clothes, looking at me, I felt, a bit askance. I determined not to think about it, that this would be one more instance of grace given, if reluctantly.

Dom Andrew spoke on patience and trust. During prayers, the abbot repeated, "Lord hear us." And we all replied, "Lord, graciously hear us."

It was just what I needed to pray. Dom Anselm was terribly kind and encouraged me to sit in the sun and sleep and read while I was here.

I woke to a noise in the middle of the night—someone going down the hall to the bathroom. I was jarred by the realization that there was no lock on my door and turned on my light for a minute although I knew that would push me into waking. Everything was more awful and terrible and wonderful then, all of my certainty and uncertainty about Jack. For hours after turning the light off, with my eyes closed, trying to sleep, I dreamed and feared, afraid and full of wonder at what my heart already knew, that my life could change so much and so suddenly.

I had prayed that I would meet someone. I had hoped I would. But I'd never imagined it would be like this—so sure.

Susan said that being here on retreat can bring to mind things one doesn't usually think about. She was mourning her brother, and Catherine was mourning a sister who'd committed suicide years ago. Somehow, in all the quiet, it was the grace of God that overwhelmed me, like my challenge here was to be able to accept good things from his hand.

Somehow Jack's goodness and God's goodness became all tied up together in my head in a way I could not entirely untangle. But the truth was, I couldn't count on Jack.

What I knew for sure was that he wasn't sure he wanted to get married—"Someday perhaps, but now?"—and that he'd just started sort of dating a girl from North Carolina and that officially we were just hanging out.

It felt like so much more than that.

I was convinced he felt the same things I did. He never said as much—like Willoughby, it was never spoken but "every day implied."[2] The way he looked at me, watched me walk down the stairs, or just paid attention to what I said. He made sure I was next to him. When we didn't have time to talk about everything, he would tell me that he wanted to hear more about what I thought later. He carried my backpack and walked on the outside of the sidewalk wherever we went, in that protective southern way.

So there was that communion, those myriad unspoken signs that exist between two people, that claim them as each other's. If he was talking to someone else when I walked in the room, I immediately had his attention. Or when I pulled on my white hoodie between classes, he reached over and rescued one of the ties that had gotten stuck inside— taking care of me, putting me right. When I'd said good-bye to Paul, I saw Jack watching while trying not to seem to be watching, to see just how close we were, like he imagined there to be competition.

People who didn't already think we were engaged assumed we were dating or that we would be soon. Everyone believed it—believed in us. Other guys noticed and kept their distance. Perhaps my active imagination generated this impression, but that was how it seemed.

So why did he send me off with this kind of uncertainty? I could only assume it was because he was uncertain himself and that I couldn't entirely trust what I felt.

Whether or not I can count on God is another question entirely. (And I feel sacrilegious just thinking that thought.) I'm not sure why the goodness and grace of God is so oppressive to me here.

The great and embarrassing disappointment of my life thus far has been the not getting married thing. Embarrassing partly because I've not been asked, never been adored like that, and partly because even in this feminist age, I still want it so much. And if that sounds crazy to some, since I'm currently thirty-three and still very marryable, it may help to know the expectations in the conservative Christian world in which I was raised. Girls were supposed to grow up, go to college, and get married. Nearly all of my friends did just that. Two of my best friends got married before our senior year in college.

So as the years went on, I worried about trying to catch up to them and their growing families and gradually came to realize—contrary to popular American Christian belief—that God does not always give you what you want.

The American Christian mentality can be a dangerous one. We are so successful, so rich, that we begin to equate these things with the blessings of God. They are great blessings, to be sure. But in some ways this leads to a faith that evaluates God's work in our lives and the lives of our friends by the amount of stuff we have received. When things work out—marriage, children, 401(k)—God is clearly present. When things do not work out, we tell ourselves and others to hold on, that God will surely come to our aid and act quickly on our behalf, bringing us what we want/need/desire/cannot live without. This is not entirely untrue; God loves to give us good things. And yet what we end up with in many ways is a faith focused on all of our riches, a faith that works only in America. Just thinking about trying to encourage Third World Christians the way we talk to each other belies the fact that these "truths" we hold on to are not universal.

Through the window of this great disappointment, my unmet longing for someone to share life with, my eyes were opened to the other side of God—the withholding side, the hard side, the side that could smite the Amalekites and keep someone in the greatest want.

I chose to believe that this harshness was still love, was still somehow for my best and would work for my good. Of course, I loved the freedom of my life. Nothing but my bank account and my calendar could stop me if I wanted to escape to the other side of the world. And truthfully I was thankful not to be responsible for a gaggle of toddlers. But somehow through this loss I grew to associate God's love with something harsh and difficult, with things that didn't feel like love at all.

As I sat on a bench under a willow tree, by the lily pond at Alton Abbey, I was immersed in sun and friendship and something like love. I felt like God was asking me to believe once again in his actual goodness, in his ability and desire to give me things that not only are good for me, but will feel good as well.

I believe that Cassandra—Jane's dear sister—would have understood my struggles with the seeming harshness of God. In one of the defining moments of Cassandra's—and by proxy, Jane's—life, her fiancé, Tom Fowle, died of yellow fever in the West Indies. He was on board a boat that belonged to Lord Craven, a friend and distant relative who had gotten him the position, who said later that he would not have allowed him to go had he realized he was engaged. The whole venture, on Tom's part, seems to have been only to help him earn enough money so he could marry Cassandra. They had been engaged for three years and were only waiting for Tom to have a better income. Lord Craven was expected to give them a comfortable church living when a position opened up. It took months for the news to reach Steventon, so in the spring of 1797, when Cassandra was expecting her dear Tom home, she learned instead of his death and burial at sea. After waiting almost five years to be able to marry, Tom was not coming home, his body sewn up in a ship's hammock and dumped over the side after what was likely a brief and perfunctory service.[3]

Because of Cassandra's careful nature, her emotions would not have been extreme. Jane said she "behave[d] with a degree of resolution & Propriety which no common mind could evince in so trying a situation,"[4] but she mourned Tom deeply and after that never seriously considered anyone else. Perhaps in part it was this tragedy that encouraged the girls into the garb of middle age sooner than was actually necessary. Jane clearly believed in marrying for love; it seems in this, as in many of her other ways of thinking about the world, she was encouraged by her sister. I wonder how her loss changed Cassandra's view of the world, her view of God. Early death was so much more common then, so much more expected, that perhaps it was not as much of a shock as it may be to us now when we hear the story retold. But Cassandra seems to have felt too strongly the harsh hand of divine justice, and I wonder if that is not a trend that started with Tom's death.

After Jane died, Cassandra wrote to her niece, "I loved her only too well, not better than she deserved, but I am conscious that my affection for her made me sometimes unjust to & negligent of others, & I can acknowledge, more than as a general principle, the justice of the hand which has struck this blow."[5] As though God were more than justified in taking Jane away at forty-one because her sister loved her too much, occasionally to the exclusion of others. I think this is so far removed from what God would have us understand of him, of the gifts he gives and takes away.

Eight

Steventon: A Solitary Walk

To walk three miles, or four miles, or five miles,
or whatever it is, above her ankles in dirt, and alone,
quite alone! what could she mean by it?
It seems to me to show an
abominable sort of conceited independence.

—MISS BINGLEY, *PRIDE AND PREJUDICE*

Jane Austen was born just here. Or actually not here exactly, but somewhere very close-by. I am a bit in awe and can't get my scattered mind to actually understand the directions in my guidebook to find the site of the rectory where the Austen family lived, where Jane was born in the terribly cold December of 1775.

I sit on a bench in the Steventon churchyard, which is very quiet, and I am blissfully alone. George Austen, Jane's father, was rector here at this sweet, small stone church, built roughly eight hundred years ago.[1] My American mind cannot fathom a building—or any place really —having survived that long. History is more mythical to me, something marvelous that happened elsewhere, that cannot be touched, only imagined. But here I sit, in the village where Jane spent her first twenty-five years,[2] next to the lane up which her father carried every baby for a public christening after he'd given the baby a private baptism at home,[3] pondering the huge yew tree in the churchyard, which Jane herself would have known, where her father hid the church key. Somewhere nearby was the hill Jane rolled down as a child, like Catherine in *Northanger Abbey*, who "loved nothing so well in the world."[4] Across from the rectory, the barn, where she threw rousing family theatricals with her brothers. And somewhere close were the elm trees she mourned after a particularly violent fall storm pulled them down.[5]

This was home. Jane loved it here. I've heard other writers describe the landscape as small, and I suppose it might be, but it seems to me everything an English country village ought to be. Houses and thatched cottages, only a couple of streets, the whole thing surrounded by gentle field- and farm-filled hills. Jane knew all of its lanes and seasons, loved its families. Her favorite subject was "3 or 4 Families in a Country Village,"[6] and Steventon no doubt provided the seeds for Longbourn and Meryton, Highbury and Uppercross.

As a child, without knowing it I think I always longed for a place to be—not any place, but my place, my home. There was no quiet village, and our house itself seemed rather too quiet, our family too small. My parents did not take kindly to my asking for additional children. Mom always said that if we had slept through the night, she would have had a dozen, but we were difficult babies, so it was just me and my brother. (My sister would join us later, which is a complicated story and not mine to tell—aren't all families complicated these days?) Our little family was plucked up every two to four years, moving from one air force assignment to the next. The only permanence we had was our love for one another and our faith—both of which, however imperfect, left me with a sense of abundance. But I longed for someplace sturdy and old, something other than Sheetrock in various shades of builder's white.

Even my home now, my town house with thinnish walls and threatening plastic pipes, feels hastily constructed, a bed in a precarious room so close to the street noises, the neighbor's diesel truck that is always in need of repair, early morning cars honking and the crashing of trash day. Herndon, the town where I live, could hardly be called a village, though we do better than other suburbs. We have concerts on the town green on Thursday and Friday nights all through the summer, a huge spring carnival with a Tilt-A-Whirl and kettle corn and over-priced tacos from the local Mexican place in May, a farmers' market every week in season. Its two distinctives, in my mind, are very bad parking lots and immigration—both legal and illegal.

Shortly after I moved in, one of the houses next door was sold to a family from El Salvador, and there were eleven or twelve of them—brothers and cousins and sisters-in-law and babies—all going in and out. I practiced my Spanish, and the guys would ask me, *"Eres casada?"* and I would try to explain, no, I wasn't married, but I just wanted to be their friend. One night Jorge, the one they call Gordito (little fat one), knocked on the door with a box almost as tall and wide as he was. I tried not to take it, but he told me he bought one for him and one for me and begged me to open it. It was a mirror, painted with a South American beach scene, all garish colors. "Plug it in, plug it in!" he said. Sure enough, it lit up and made noises—birds calling and the whoosh whoosh whoosh of waves. I wondered if somehow he thought I loved him because I couldn't figure out how to tactfully give it back. And they would ask, "You live there by yourself? Where's your family?" It made no sense to them. I would hear them every weekend—occasionally throwing empty beer bottles into the trees, but mostly just being together, eating and laughing and talking.

As a child, no matter where we were, we went to my aunt and uncle's home in upstate New York every Thanksgiving. This meant long, late drives in the station wagon with my brother and me in sleeping bags in the back or layovers in airports with comic books and art caddies in tow. Ginny and Steve's home, though technically it was in just another suburb, had solidity—hardwood floors and a fireplace, with a woven rug, cream wallpaper in the dining room with a pattern of soft blue velvet, and a basement of cold gray cement. There would be waffles in the morning with bacon, and if we were lucky—and we usually were—snow.

They would drive us to see Ice Capades, and Uncle Steve would look at the girls through his binoculars, which seemed a little creepy, and then take us to a diner for ice cream sundaes. We went shopping in the city and came home with stuffed animals and bags of gold chocolate coins. And on Thanksgiving, we always got dressed up and had dinner on the good china, with the silver and the sparkly glasses, and maybe a cardinal would have his own feast on the bird feeder outside the sliding glass doors. On summer trips there was lemonade and snapdragons, picnics in great forests, and trips to see Niagara Falls. Their home became one of my Most Important Places, a place that always smelled the same, that was older than I was, somewhere secure.

There is a place you belong. Maybe that's what all of us want to know. Maybe that's one reason we love Jane's books so much. They put us into little villages, places where everyone knows everyone and is known in turn, with a kind of familiarity we have largely lost.

I cannot get the church door to open. A guy running his hounds through the neighboring field (they really should not wear shorts when they are so very white—especially with black socks) tells me it should be open, but I push and pull on the iron handles to no avail. The bugs and birds are quietly raucous. The sun is bright, and there is a little misting rain and a few high clouds, but I am determined that it will be fine. I have four glorious solitary hours, and I intend to head out across the fields Jane knew in search of her dear friend Anne Lefroy's house, with "a sort of conceited independence"[7] of which even Lizzy would be proud.

My book says, "Walk over the field towards the copse."[8] I do not know exactly what a copse is. And how, in the middle of the countryside, am I to choose which one to walk toward?

⚜

By all accounts, the Austen family was a rather remarkable family to be part of. It was built on George and Cassandra's love for each other, which seems to have been warm and genuine. Once, when the boys were small, Cassandra went to help her sister in childbirth, and George wrote to his sister-in-law, "I don't much like this lonely kind of Life," and when he talked about the family possibly paying a visit, he said, "I say we, for I certainly shall not let my Wife come alone, & I dare say she will not leave her children behind her."[9] You can just see the country rector, who did not marry until he was almost thirty-three,[10] in his rather plain small house, missing his dear wife. George had a wonderful disposition, described as "bright & hopeful."[11] Cassandra, who loved to write small, witty poems, seems to have been full of life.

The Austens were a family that talked about things. There was much intelligent conversation and a great deal of laughter. George was made a fellow at St. John's in Oxford after finishing his divinity degree.[12]

He could have stayed on there, but he gave up academic life for this—a small parish, a dairy, a poultry yard, a walled vegetable garden surrounded by fruit trees, a weather vane that creaked in the wind, and a houseful of children.[13]

George also ran Cheesedown Farm[14] on the north side of the parish to help make ends meet and for nearly twenty-five years ran a small school for boys out of the Austen home, which, though rather plain, had seven bedrooms upstairs and three attics.[15]

There were eight "very good Children,"[16] six boys and two girls—James, George, Edward, Henry, Cassandra, Frank, Jane, and Charles. James was a scholar who followed in his father's footsteps almost exactly. When Jane was just three,[17] he left for Oxford, joined the church, and eventually became rector of Steventon. George, the second oldest, was mentally disabled in some way and had fits. It's possible he was deaf and dumb.[18] Many people who talk about the Austen family say there were only seven children, and I think it is because they are forgetting George. The Austens kept him at home for a while but eventually sent him to live in a neighboring village with a family that cared for Mrs. Austen's younger brother, who struggled with similar difficulties.

Edward was sharp and lovable, with a head more for business than Latin, and wound up being adopted by wealthy cousins and inheriting their estates. Charming, good-looking, and energetic, Henry was Jane's favorite. Active little Frank and Charles set off for the Royal Naval Academy at age twelve and eleven and began navy life in their early teens, sometimes leaving England for years at a time to sail to the Far East, the Mediterranean, Bermuda, and the West Indies, eventually both becoming admirals. (Frank actually left for his first tour of duty in the East Indies when he was just fourteen and wouldn't return home for five years.)

We know that in their adult years, the siblings all genuinely respected one another, that there was a great deal of friendship and camaraderie. Jane must have been thinking of her own brothers and sister when she wrote in *Mansfield Park* that the fraternal bond could be stronger than even the conjugal. "Children of the same family, the same blood, with the same first associations and habits, have some means of enjoyment in their power, which no subsequent connections can supply," she wrote.[19]

Their cousin Eliza wrote of the "uncommon Abilities, which indeed seem to have been bestowed, tho' in a different way, upon each Member of this Family."[20] The Austen parents seem to have been incredibly good at channeling their children's energies into the areas where their natural strengths lay. There seem not to have been undue parental expectations that the children would turn out one way or another, or choose a particular career, and this underlying sense of freedom must have played a role in the choices Jane made—in her writing and choosing not to marry.

Jane was closest to Cassandra, her elder sister by three years. They had an incredibly tight bond and "seemed to lead a life to themselves within the general family life, which was shared only by each other."[21] Cassandra was no doubt the more practical, the more complying. Jane the more emotional, creative, and at times serious. Their nephew James Edward described Cassandra as "always prudent and well judging, but with less outward demonstration of feeling and less sunniness of temper than Jane possessed,"[22] which makes me think their own relationship could have been to some extent a model for Elinor and Marianne's in *Sense and Sensibility.* (James Edward said this was impossible since Jane had not Marianne's failings. I expect, though, that she had enough to easily imagine greater.)

I have come to view my own family as a bit remarkable, precisely because, like the Austens, we talk about things and laugh a great deal. All we need is a meal and a bottle of wine, and we have hours of entertainment. And underneath everything is a great deal of love. I haven't always seen things this way, and perhaps we have not always been remarkable, but we grew up well, I suppose, now that we are finally in our thirties and approximating adulthood.

⚜

Jane was a great walker, and I guess I may make some claim to the title. In *Pride and Prejudice,* she probably wrote Lizzy's experiences out of her own, "crossing field after field at a quick pace, jumping over stiles and springing over puddles with impatient activity...with weary ankles, dirty stockings, and a face glowing with the warmth of exercise."[23] That describes me wandering alone through the Hampshire countryside— with small amounts of terror thrown in.

The walking directions from my book are, in fact, crazy. "Cross the railway,"[24] it says, neglecting to mention the fifty yards of weeds and brambles. "Keep the pines close on your right"[25]—this in a near forest. Path markers are relatively small, sometimes no more than a three-by-three sign on a fence post, and if there are bigger signs, they are wood, making them difficult to see. Stiles—for clambering over fences—are often just a few pieces of board stuck at funny angles with just enough support to enable a foothold.

The path crosses private property, occasionally beside fields of livestock. Friesian cows, hogging the shade, followed me with their glassy eyes. A pony with a red leather fringe tied around his head (to keep the flies off?) tramps after me along his fence, the whole time goofily eying my banana.

I have not always been a great walker. On my thirteenth birthday, my parents took the family down to the Mall in D.C.—we had just moved there—and we walked the entire thing in the October sun. When we got to the Lincoln Memorial, I refused to climb the steps because I had walked quite far enough and because I was now a teenager and growingly annoyed to be with my entire family in public, walking around like tourists. I got over that—or most of it at least.

Something my father said once changed my life. I was telling him that one of my dreams was to meet the writer Madeleine L'Engle, and he said, "Well, what are you going to do to make that happen?"

Something inside me snapped—in the best possible way. I suppose there had been a growing realization that if I did nothing but think about doing things—like meeting Madeleine L'Engle—I would grow old having actually done nothing. The things I expected—the marriage and kids—had not come, and anything else that was going to happen I had to make happen myself. So I signed up for a writers' retreat at a convent with Madeleine L'Engle for three years in a row. She broke her hip and then was unable to travel for various reasons and then stopped traveling all together, so I never met her, but I came very close. Then I went to Paris completely on my own, with just the barest of French, just because I dreamed of a romantic solo trip. I saw the roses in Rodin's garden in full bloom and the water lilies and irises at Giverny, went to the ballet at the Palais Garnier opera house, and saw hundreds of Monet's water lily paintings in a special exhibit at Musée de l'Orangerie, serendipitously ending up in a hotel room with a view of the Eiffel Tower.

A couple of years later, I was telling my friend Dee, "One of my dreams is to hike the Grand Canyon."

She said, "Really? Want to go over Thanksgiving?"

And there was that moment when I thought, *I can either do this or not—I can live my dreams, or I can just talk about them.* So I went. At twenty-seven I bought a pack and a water filter and broke in my hiking boots for fifty miles before we left and learned the intricacies of going to the bathroom off-trail (one of my all-time greatest fears) in a place where you have to pack out absolutely all (really, *all*) of your trash. We slept on a ledge in one of the side canyons, under a nearly full moon, and walked all the way down to the Colorado River and all the way back up, feeling like we knew parts of the Canyon intimately—its quietness and shades, hot afternoons and freezing nights.

Two years later I was carrying nearly forty pounds, walking into a thick Montana forest for seven days in Glacier National Park back country. I was afraid of bears there, the way I had been of scorpions and rattlesnakes in the Canyon, or that maybe I would die somehow on the trail—starved to death with a broken leg, happening upon a big grizzly in her dawn feeding. There are always fears. Maybe for some people there aren't, but I am not one of those people. C. S. Lewis said every time you make a decision, you change the central part of you that chooses.[26] He meant moral choices—whenever you choose to lie, for example, or not to lie, you change the substance of who you are and what you are likely to do the next time you have a choice to make. I think the same is true, though, with our lives. Every time you make a decision—to live your life, to do the things that call you—you change what you are likely to do the next time you have a choice.

So I'm wondering which row of pine trees to keep on my right, praying desperately that I don't get lost. (Sheesh. I make it sound like I am exploring somewhere when in fact I'm in rural England, with a mobile phone and a PowerBar, in white cropped pants with a green T-shirt and matching shoes.)

I think the countryside must look something like it did in Jane's day. Walking through the fields, I begin to feel human again, the exertion somehow helping me recover from exhaustion. I have to stop every now and then just to take it all in, to wonder and feel giddy and pray.

"Walk ahead over a large field aiming for the left-hand corner of a strip of woodland,"[27] the guide says. *Aim left through a large field?* I think. But when I cross a stile under the trees, I find a field full of high summer wheat, with a green walking path cut through the middle, aiming for the left corner.

I walk into the field and stop in the sun. I don't think these are the paths Jane walked, of course. But I imagine this may be the way she felt walking them: gloriously alone, surrounded by the heat and health of nature, with friends waiting at the other end.

⚜

An hour and a half of walking takes me to lovely Ashe House, on a quiet lane. The entire village of Ashe appears to consist of this little street with brick homes and gardens and the church. Ashe House is a simple Georgian structure, red brick with a row of front windows and a fanlight above the door, vines and roses climbing along the front. It looks like the perfect house—tasteful and simple but quietly grand—and would have been dear to Jane as the home of her friend. It's rumored that Tom Lefroy chased Jane through the garden here.

Anne Lefroy was more than a friend; she was like a mentor to Jane. She was twenty-six years Jane's senior and met Jane when she was seven—just a girl, but a smart girl who already loved literature. Madam Lefroy, as she was known, was intelligent and kind. She loved poetry, taught the village children to read and write, and personally vaccinated the entire neighborhood for smallpox.[28] She was beautiful and gracious. Her husband was rector here at Ashe Church.

I can imagine the influence she had on Jane's life, this lovely woman who lived out her faith among the poor, who loved those around her with more than words, and who could also meaningfully discuss poets and playwrights. She was strong in an age in which women were not thought to be so, educated when most women were not. She must have had a streak of independence as well. I think Jane learned something from her about the possibilities of life, of what it could be like to be a woman who was strong and yet not improperly so, about the purposes and value of wealth not for its own sake but as it might be used for the sake of others. Anne's values would have been much like George and Cassandra Austen's, but sometimes these things are easier caught from those who are not your parents.

We all must strike a certain balance, which I tend to think of when I am in ballet and my foot must be more pointed, my legs more turned out, my heel back, stomach held in, the proper triangle between my outstretched arms and solar plexus, and the whole thing stretching up, up, up, like I am pulled by a string. It is never right; there will always be adjustments. But all of us have this balance in our lives, attempting to work out our faith within our particular cultural context. We must be more humble (or perhaps I should say I must be) yet use our strength and maintain compassion when we are bombarded with needs in a world where everyone now is our neighbor and we know everyone's tragic stories. Anne's balance was to stretch within her late-eighteenth-century world where women's roles were so limited, where the Christian faith was often in name only, where it would have been more than acceptable for her to learn nothing and do nothing. But—continuing this analogy—she danced.

I'm thankful to have had dance instructors of my own, chief among them Beth, whom I think of as kind of my own Anne Lefroy. She is lovely and probably the best natural communicator I know. Beth is fourteen years my senior, and her oldest daughter fourteen years my junior, and I believe I met her when I was fifteen or sixteen. I would come to clean her house every week, and little two-year-old Anna would follow me around to help, but it was never so much about cleaning as it was about building a relationship. Our families melded together in a way—we went to the same church, and Mom watched her kids every week, and over years of holidays and simpler days we grew close. I held all of her five children when they were small, and she has heard all of my love stories. She will always be like family, one of the people I count on to help me understand where the balance of my life is off and how to correct it.

Anne interfered a bit with Jane's love life—not always in the most welcome ways. She was the one who sent Tom home, of course, when there seemed to be a growing attachment, and she was the one who encouraged the somewhat ridiculous Samuel Blackall. I think perhaps *Persuasion*'s Lady Russell, who keeps Anne from Wentworth once and later encourages the duplicitous Mr. Elliot, may have been partly based on Madam Lefroy. She died tragically in a riding accident on Jane's twenty-ninth birthday, when her horse got away from her and she fell off. Jane wrote a poem in her memory, speaking of her "solid Worth" and "captivating Grace."[29] She was not perfect, but she was wonderful. If there are traces of Madam Lefroy in Lady Russell, I do not think she could have rivaled the "genuine warmth of heart without pretence"[30] of Jane's dear friend.

I stop for a moment simply to remember Anne in the Ashe churchyard, by the moss-covered Lefroy graves. It is peaceful and sheltered, gated with intricate wood arches, and shaded by trees.

Nine

Chawton: Love and Grit

Home could not be faultless.

—PRIDE AND PREJUDICE

One of my favorite images of Jane is that of her sitting by the fire with her mom and their neighbor Miss Benn, reading *Pride and Prejudice* after it had just come out—the already best-selling novelist reading her new book (the one she called "my own darling Child"[1]) out loud with her mother, who couldn't get the voices right, and their old neighbor friend. Jane never put her own name on any of her books—a lady never would—so when *Sense and Sensibility* came out, it said only, *By A Lady*[2] (except some of the printers misprinted it to read *By Lady A.,* which created some speculation in society about other ladies with last names beginning in *A*), and when *Pride and Prejudice* came out, it said, *By the Author of Sense and Sensibility.* She hoped to keep her authorship a secret, and she and her mother endeavored to hide the source of their enthusiasm for the new novel, but it seems Miss Benn quickly guessed that they were more than just interested readers.

I sit in the abbey, in my favorite spot at the desk by the bay window looking out on the garden, thinking over everything I have seen today—

the topaz crosses[3] that Jane scolded Charles for buying for her and Cassandra, Mrs. Austen's red riding habit (which she wore when she got married and for two years following, because she could not afford another dress, then made into a coat for little Frank for his boyish hunting exploits),[4] a quilt Cassandra and Jane and their mother made, a lace collar Jane herself made, some of her small, perfect handwriting—neat and elegant—a lock of her hair (faded) and a lock of her father's hair (white), the small bedroom she and Cassandra shared (twelve by twelve?), her writing table by the bay window in the dining room. The table is tiny, small angles all around the top, on a little pedestal, not what I expected, and I thought she wrote in the drawing room and not the dining room. But there it was, in the dining room with the squeaky door so she could put her writing away if she heard anyone coming.

Chawton Cottage, the cottage Jane and her mom and sister shared along with their dear friend Martha Lloyd—where she sat by the fire reading her darling *P&P*—is now Jane Austen's House Museum, restored to look the way it did when they lived there and full of family things. Chawton was Edward's estate, and the cottage was his gift to his mother and sisters after his father died. Well, not a gift exactly, but he let them live there. It's where Jane lived when her work began to be published, where she wrote or edited almost every story. Truthfully, the cottage looks like a big brick box, but it's quaint inside and the flower gardens are lovely.

I talked Susan and Lane and Catherine, my friends from the abbey, into coming with me today. (Or rather, they offered because they have been graciously driving me all around, public transportation in the Hampshire countryside being slightly difficult.) We went first to St. Nicholas Church—a different St. Nicholas, this one on the grounds of Chawton

House. It was a living Jane's brother Henry wanted, and Edward offered to buy it for him (because church positions were bought and sold then), but Mr. Papillon, to whom it had been promised—and whom some family members were always expecting to propose to Jane, which was a great joke—was not willing to give it up.[5] There were huge round sheep in the field outside, unshorn, with a few little ones too. We spent half an hour reading all the gravestones of the various Edward and Elizabeth Knights and found the graves for Jane's mom and Cassandra.

Edward seems to have been officially adopted into the Knight family when he was fifteen or sixteen, though he had been singled out by them much earlier.[6] Thomas and Catherine Knight were distant cousins of Mr. Austen. They came through Hampshire on their honeymoon and enjoyed young Edward, then just twelve, so much that they took him with them for part of their trip. (Which sounds very strange to us, but it was not unusual to have other friends or family on a wedding tour then.)

When it became clear that they wouldn't have children of their own, they began inviting him for holidays, which Mr. Austen grudgingly allowed, fearing Edward would get behind on his Latin grammar. But gradually it became evident that they wanted to adopt Edward and that he would not need his Latin grammar much longer. It was incredibly advantageous, landing Edward in a completely different realm of society. Edward wasn't eager to get away from his real family, so it was years before he went to live with the Knights permanently, and he waited until his adopted father and mother died before taking on the Knight name along with his inheritance.[7]

So Edward inherited the Chawton estate—the great house and lands—another huge estate in Kent called Godmersham, and the

Steventon estate, including the manor house just down the lane from the rectory in which he'd grown up. He lived worlds away from the rest of the Austens, in wealth and privilege. It seems strange to think of one child inheriting so much when even his parents were merely surviving for the most part, but great discrepancies among families were fairly regular. Among the wealthy, the first son would inherit all the father's estates. The second would inherit from the mother's side of the family, if any wealth existed there, and the rest were expected to make it on their own—the daughters to marry well, the sons to join the army or study law or join the church.

Still, it must have been a bit awkward for everyone.

While the others studied—James and Henry at Oxford, Frank and Charles at the naval academy—Edward went on a four-year-long grand tour in the tradition of wealthy sons. We can't trace his route exactly, but we know he went to Switzerland and Rome at the least and probably spent a year studying in Germany.[8]

The Austen family, as kind and lively as they were, had their hints of dysfunction. Is any family without them? There are always small aggressions, and whoever we are at our core—tainted by insecurity, pride, and jealousy—all of that comes out, and these character faults rub against one another.

It seems that James, the oldest, could be a bit demanding and officious. His second wife, Mary Lloyd, who had been a good friend of the girls, ended up being unable to control her jealousy. She could not stand the fact that James had been married before (his first wife died young) or that he had courted their lovely cousin Eliza. She was a force of negativity and hardly treated her stepdaughter, Anna, as a member of the family. James, showing himself to be weak, ignored his daughter

Anna so as not to anger his new wife and never again mentioned Anna's dear mother.[9] Mrs. Austen may have had a talent for imagining herself ill.[10] Charming Henry had some difficulty making his way in the world and at one point went bankrupt, losing valuable family holdings.[11] Mr. Austen could be impetuous.

The Chawton Cottage may be another example of a small tear in the family fabric. After Mr. Austen died, it was expected that the brothers would help take care of Mrs. Austen, Cassandra, and Jane, as their income was much reduced. They went to live with Frank awhile in Southampton until his small family began to grow and they felt they should no longer impose. They visited relatives. They took lower accommodations in Bath. Edward—who should most have been able to afford it—seems to have been slow in offering significant support. He waited until after his wife died to give his mother and sisters Chawton Cottage. (His wife seems to have adored Cassandra and been rather uncomfortable with Jane, so perhaps there was something keeping him back.) Jane and Cassandra always thought of Edward as kind and gracious. People wonder if *Emma*'s Mr. Knightley was in some way fashioned after the brother who took the name of Knight. So perhaps I am misreading the situation. We know that there was some anxiety about where the girls and their mother would live and what they could afford, and this was finally removed when they were able to settle here in Chawton.

Whatever irritations there were in the Austen family—and somehow it is reassuring to read Jane's letters, even the ones Cassandra thought were completely safe, and get some hint of them—the girls lived with them. Like my neighbors from El Salvador, they were driven by society and situation to need their family and to always be with them. It was certainly not a fair society—women would rarely have inherited wealth, and it would have been unthinkable for the Knights to bestow their estates on one of the Austen girls. And the girls seem to have lived at the beck and call of their brothers, coming to visit them for months when a new baby arrived, taking care of their children whenever necessary. We could never endure this kind of dependence today, and certainly it led to all kinds of evils in families where there was little love. But with the Austens, there was a great deal of love, however imperfect, and the arrangement, rather than creating resentment, seems to have given them assurance and created their own little world, which, while they lived at Chawton, they had little desire to leave.

There are people who love you. I think that's another thing all of us want to know. For those of us who are lucky, that begins with our families, whatever kind of irritating grit there may be underneath.

⚜

Chawton Great House (now a library for the study of early English women writers) is perfect for ghosts—grand and heavy, with thick oak paneling going back to the Elizabethan era, and stone floors. It just so happens that there are two ghosts, one known for going up and down one of the many sets of stairs. Our tour guide had seen him. I don't particularly ever wish to see a ghost—or an angel for that matter—but there is something delicious about imagining them (which, of course, little Catherine Morland of *Northanger Abbey* would understand).

We have an abundance of ghosts in Virginia from all of our brutal Civil War ground. One of my favorite stories involves a friend of my brother who was housesitting. In the middle of the night, she heard something and woke up to find the ghost of a Civil War soldier in her room. He had a beard, and he was blue, I think (which makes it sound very funny. A blue ghost?). She would have thought she was imagining things if the cat and the dog weren't hissing and snarling, hair raised. So she called 911. And he just stood there, smiling an evil grin at her the whole time she called. When her friends got back, they said, "Oh yeah, he only shows up when there's a woman alone in the house."

I absolutely love this story, until I am alone in my room in the dark and start to fear that my own delicious imaginings could summon the evil smiling soldier, so then I pray that God will surround me with angels to protect me and that I will not have to see any of *them* either.

❧

Jane wrote three evening prayers. In one of them she talks about the blessings of God, thanking him and asking that they will continue, understanding that she was never worthy of them in the first place. She says, "We feel that we have been blessed far beyond any thing that we have deserved; and though we cannot but pray for a continuance of all these mercies, we acknowledge our unworthiness of them and implore thee to pardon the presumption of our desires."[12]

I read that and felt terribly insecure. *Oh, dear God, you have given abundant blessings. I do not deserve them, and I cannot help but ask for more.* I am sure this is not what Jane intended, but at the moment I do not feel secure in the whims of God. All these blessings—this sense of love and happiness, which I have not felt for so long (not that Jack is the only source of that, far from it)—are they going to continue? I feel a little like I am begging. I do not know how he will respond.

My heart and mind are far from consistent. I will be the first to admit that. As much as I fear God, I have come to expect great gifts from him—and small gifts as well—and feel so assured of encountering them now, on this trip.

The other day I crossed the fields into the village of Deane, where both George and James Austen were rector at one point, where the Harwoods lived, and where Jane and her brothers and sister attended balls. I was writing down the number for the rector, to call to see if he could get me into St. Nicholas in Steventon, when a van pulled up with a sign on the back that said Hidden Britain Tours. Phil and Sue Howe were putting together—of all things—a Jane Austen tour of Hampshire. They had just been to St. Nicholas and drove me back there (the door was unlocked the whole time, but I didn't know how to open it) so that I was able to sit in the small pews for a few minutes and wonder at the gorgeous paintings on the walls, which look like an ancient sort of wallpaper, in simple dark reds and greens, flowers and vines, but painted on. Then they drove me to Oakley Hall, home of Mrs. Augusta Bramston, who thought Jane's writing was "downright nonsense,"[13] and on to Manydown, which was the seat of the Bigg-Wither family and would have been Jane's home had she been willing to marry for money rather than love. Unfortunately, the house is no longer standing.

Phil and I spent time comparing notes on Jane and both tried to figure out again where the Steventon rectory was, to no avail. Now I have reread the guidebook, and it basically says to walk down the road from the church, and the rectory was across the street on the left.[14] (Sheesh! I'm dying to go back and see it.) But it was a great serendipitous blessing just happening to run into them.

Then there are the monks and the great peace of the abbey—the lovely garden and the care they take of me, whom they do not know at all. I'm sad to be leaving them and sadder that I haven't gotten to know them better. I find myself wondering about them, what they are like, wishing I could talk to them. The only time I see them is during meals, which are silent, and after night prayers they glide out with their hoods up, in silence that will last until morning. Occasionally, if I am around, I might catch them having coffee after morning mass and they will stop and chat, at least a few of them, before they rush off to make icons or organize retreats.

I know very little about them for certain. The abbot, who appears to be in his sixties, has lived here nearly forty years. He wears sandals that look like Teva's and squeak on the tile floor. He has a big bushy beard and carries around a bandanna, and I imagine him to be a hippie sort of a monk, if that's possible. I have taken to studying the shoes carefully because there is so little else that distinguishes them from one another.

Dom Nicholas, who was so careful to warn me about the shower mat, wears the sort of comfortable, sensible black shoes you would expect of him. Kind Anselm, the renowned iconographer, is thin and careful with his trim gray beard and studious spectacles. He wears nice black leather. There is a new one (well, not new to them, but to me). He is Welsh, with short dark hair, and wears what look sort of like Doc Martens. He seems to be second in command and sings and reads as though he ought to read loudly, not as though it is a performance exactly, but he is much more expressive than the others, which is a bit unsettling after getting used to the comforting monotone, where everyone blends together.

Isn't it funny that at a monastery, where everything appears to be the same, their shoes hint at an individuality underneath everything?

One of my favorites is Father Timothy. Dress shoes again. He has only ever said two words to me, I think, and that was tonight during dinner when everyone was, of course, silent. I was trying to eat as quickly as possible because the whole thing is intimidating to me, and they eat very fast (perhaps so they can get back to their prayers), and then I find them watching me finish and decide it's just easier to stop. The other night as everyone was finishing up last bits and pieces, I grabbed a little plum and started to eat it the way I always do, taking small bites around the pit—but plums are messy and so perhaps this is better done without an audience and not in a silent room. I hadn't fully realized until that moment that I had never seen any of the rest of them biting into any sort of fruit. They slice and eat them with the utmost civility. Nor had I realized that eating a plum might be a sensuous thing. But there I was, in the silence, with the messy, suddenly sexy fruit. I am sure I broke the Benedictine code. I will have to look this up.

So Father Timothy, the gardener, sits next to me and takes care of me during meals. I believe this is his assignment. Sometimes he adds more to my plate just when he sees I've finished something if it seems to be something I really like. Mostly he just offers me anything on the table I could want whenever something starts to look low. He has the kindest face, and by looking at him, I would have to say, the most active mind. I would love to know what he's thinking about or have a theological discussion with him. Tonight at dinner (which was only bread and cheese and peanut butter because Wednesday is fast day), he kept peering over. I offered him the fruit bowl, which he didn't want, but he kept craning, staring intently at something, until finally, with the quietest voice and the best British accent, he leaned over and said, "More tea?" I believe those are the only two words he's said to me, though I feel like I know him.

Then there is Andrew, the biggest mystery. He does not wear shoes at all. He walks with a cane and wears thick glasses, the kind that sort of distort the eyes when you're looking at them. His thin hair, which has receded, is shaved. He has a wicked wit and one of the nicest voices I've ever heard, deep and comforting. Sunday, when I first arrived, he spoke at mass on patience and trust.

That night over dinner—one of the only meals where speaking was allowed—I told him, "You were speaking to me."

He said, "I was speaking to myself. I always preach to myself." As though none of us are alone in the things we struggle with. I think he said he's been here twenty years.

Has he never worn shoes in all that time? And how do he and Nicholas and Anselm, who seem so different, get along? They read the psalm the other night about brothers living together in unity, and I hope they do.

And tonight was the greatest gift. Susan remembered the other day, as we were walking around Chawton, that her neighbor is a distant relative of Jane's—or rather a distant relative of Edward Austen Knight since Jane had no children. So after dinner I grabbed my notebook and recorder, and Susan picked me up to spend an evening with her neighbor and his wife. It seemed like it could be such an intrusion—the American tourist, showing up with all of her questions—but they were so gracious.

On September 16, 1813, Jane wrote to her sister, Cassandra, from London about going with Edward to the Wedgwood store in London, where he picked out his china.[15] It was designed especially for him, a geometric pattern of purple and gold around the edge, with an image of the gray friar, which was the family's crest. They have some at the Jane Austen House, of course, with signs saying DO NOT TOUCH. Sam and his wife have some on a shelf on their wall, and as I was staring in awe, he said, "Here, go ahead," and handed me a small tureen.

Sam is one of the kindest, most down-to-earth people I've ever met. He enjoys his legacy, I guess, but doesn't make a big deal of it and doesn't really want it made a big deal of. He kept asking to make sure I wouldn't write about the things he was saying (a promise I have already broken), so I put my recorder and notebook away and just listened. I hope he will forgive me. He said he doesn't really know anything about Austen.

He showed me some framed maps on vellum of the Chawton lands (lands of Thomas Knight Esq., father of the Thomas Knight who adopted Edward) dated 1741, with some fields labeled "Jane's fields." He said the folks at Chawton today might tell you that is because Jane loved to walk in them, but that can't be true because Jane wasn't born in 1741 and they were already called that.

He had a copy of the gorgeous family coat of arms, with the Knight, Austen, Leigh, and Perrot symbols and the gray friar on top (and now I understand why the pub in town is called the Greyfriar). He said Jane probably sat in the chair I was sitting in, which was from the great house, but they'd had it recovered so she hadn't sat on that part of it. And he showed me an elegant dining-room chair that lifted up to reveal a chamber pot underneath and said she probably *did* use that, but I overcame my urge to touch all things Austen. Just before we headed out, Susan asked about the board of old skeleton keys hanging up on the wall above the chair I'd been sitting in, and Sam said they were mostly from the old house, and then he handed me two engraved "Godmersham Park," from Edward's estate outside of Canterbury.

So these are my gifts. Astounding and simple. The kindness of strangers, abundant roses and lavender in the garden, a quiet monk asking if I wouldn't like more tea, a distant relative of dear Jane. I hold on to them and ponder them, like beads on a rosary, waiting for more.

Ten

London: To Friends

Friendship is certainly the finest balm
for the pangs of disappointed love.

— *Northanger Abbey*

So many people have loved me unconditionally in my life, more than I have deserved. I guess that is part of the definition of unconditional love, that it does not depend on our deserving it. So I am off to the London suburbs and to Margaret, who is one of those who loves me no matter what.

Perhaps I will regret getting on the train. On the other hand, perhaps I will be blown up and won't be capable of regretting anything. I was beginning to think that I would go crazy if I attempted to live for long with all the quiet and all the prayer of the monastery—I think maybe it is possible to pray too much, or maybe that is the kind of life that must be gradually worked into, and my prayer muscles are terribly weak. But just as I was saying good-bye to Dom Nicholas, with the cab waiting, Dom Andrew said, "There's something happening in London. Be careful."

We listened to the radio in the cab and discovered that it was another series of bombs that sounded like a copycat attempt from the bombing two weeks ago, when terrorists walked onto the Tube in rush hour and blew themselves up. This one doesn't sound like it's been so successful. *At least,* I thought, *I am only going on the train today and not on the Tube.* And if I stayed in Hampshire, how long would I have waited? How would I know it was safe to travel? I can't just wait in the country for all threat of terrorism to be gone. It's a bit nerve-racking all the same—there's a prickly awareness to traveling now—but the trains are full, so everyone must have come to the same conclusion I did.

How do I explain Margaret? I have come to think of her as something like my English gran, though she might be surprised to know that, and I hardly get to see her (and really she's not old enough to be my grandmother). She talks half as much as Miss Bates and much more intelligently, which makes her an ideal companion. Actually, the last time we got together was on September 11—*the* September 11. I was having her over for dinner, and in spite of everything, I thought, *Well, we can't watch news about the disaster all the time,* so I drove out to her daughter's and picked her up. I made her one of my favorite things: BLTs with garden-fresh tomatoes. I asked if they had BLTs in England, thinking I was offering her an American summer tradition, and she said something like, "Well yes, you know, in vending machines." And I made her truly horrible tea (because Americans really know nothing about how to make good tea), which she said she rather liked, and served fresh berries with cream and brown sugar.

Margaret is desperately afraid of flying, which makes things complicated, since one of her daughters and three of her granddaughters live in Virginia and she lives in England. We talked about how the last time she flew in to the States, the pilot let her come up into the cockpit to see because they all knew how afraid she was, and how she got to see the whole city of New York from the air, spread out below her—including the Towers, suddenly gone.

If things are going to blow up every time we get together, I hope our meetings will be few and far between. But perhaps I should just hope that things will stop blowing up.

How I know Margaret may be rather complicated to someone on the outside. To me she just feels like family. Her daughter and son-in-law, Gill and Mark, have lived in Virginia for years and worked with my youth group when I was growing up. I guess they were in their twenties then, probably younger than I am now. I was twelve.

Our church met in an elementary school on blue chairs in the cafeteria. There were about 150 of us then. We sang hymns and choruses. The pastor preached—and still does—bullet-point sermons through books of the Bible, verse by verse. Every month we had a big potluck, and Jeannie would make her spaghetti salad, and Mrs. Turner would make minicheesecakes, and we kids would sit on our own, playing drinking games without the alcohol, which seemed ridiculously fun.

I have yet to fully replicate this kind of community in my adult life. There was no question that this was family. The music talent was questionable (and I have to implicate myself when I say that, because of course I took the opportunity to sing my favorite songs to backup tracks—*eesh*), and eventually I grew away from this particular nondenominational, independent way of looking at the world. But this is where I learned to mean my faith, to study Scripture and put forth my own well-thought-out (or, at times, not so much) perspectives, to love people and live in community. And I received a boatload of love. In some ways still, more than anyplace else, this is home.

So Mark and Gill, who helped lead Bible studies and ran the drama team and went on retreats with us, were part of my growing-up years. In college, when my parents and I did our minitour of Europe after I had spent the summer studying in Spain, we stayed with Gill's mom and dad, Margaret and Jack, and met her sisters and their husbands. I have a feeling I was a bit sullen, but Margaret opened her home and reached out to all of us with an unconditional, "Here, are you comfortable? I thought I would make a roast for dinner. Would you like some tea?" And she and Jack drove us to Anne Boleyn's childhood home, Hever Castle, one day, where we wandered through the gardens and stopped somewhere in the country for a pub lunch. They always fought about the driving, Margaret and Jack, and I loved that about them.

My own extended family is tiny—just Grammy and some cousins we haven't done well keeping in touch with. I feel remarkably lucky—or rather blessed—to have another extended family of a different kind.

❧

I've been thinking about Jane and all of her steady friendships—Martha Lloyd, the Bigg sisters, Anne Lefroy. She knew the same people all her life. (On the other hand, she was also to some degree stuck with the same people all her life.) My friendships shift with what sometimes feels like alarming frequency, sometimes painfully so, regenerating themselves like skin cells or taste buds so that you fear that seven years from now your group of friends will not look the same as it does today. Dear people move in and out; we no longer move in the same circles or see things quite the same way. Sudden changes sometimes, other times just slowly growing in different directions. Sometimes there is no emotional distance at all, only physical separation, but always some level of grief, some question about whether there will be more who understand me or whether I will just be alone. I've heard that saying about choosing your friends, but I think most of my great friendships have just happened to me. Some are easy and fun, some are serious, some feel slightly askew between seasons of nearness.

There are college friends who will be close the rest of my life—sweet Brenda, who used to sing praise songs with me on the steps of South Hall and loved to talk late into the night about the theological mysteries of angels while I was falling asleep, or Diane, whom I've actually known since first grade, the only friend I've had nearly all my life. I remember as a child she was always neat, and I was the one with a wrinkled uniform with my maroon knee socks rolled down to my ankles. And Beth in Ohio with her four kids and doctor-husband. (Beth who snuck out the window with me when we were both RAs to see said doctor-husband—boyfriend then—and his friends on a naked midnight run. Sadly, we ended up hiding in the bushes for an hour, all anticipation and—honestly—partly dread, while security drove back and forth, which is probably a good thing. I'm not sure how my virgin eyes would have reacted to a whole group of naked Christian college boys.)

After college I had a tough time settling into a family of friends. Bev and Jordan and Clare were all gifts of friendships, sent my way when I didn't know I needed them. Clare, my roommate, came to me through a friend of mine who was an acquaintance of a friend of a friend of Clare's, or something like that. She needed a place to stay for an eight-week summer internship, and I was unemployed and had prayed for a roommate to help with the mortgage, but I didn't have any idea where I would find one. Though we'd never met, I figured I could put up with anything for eight weeks, and so did she. But when she moved in, we found out we were eerily similar—thoughtful, passionate about faith but uncomfortable with much of evangelical Christianity, Anglophiles, fans of C. S. Lewis and Madeleine L'Engle and Jane Austen, prone to depression, shy, and feeling like our first impressions are generally bad. Clare is messier than I am, and perhaps slightly more prone to depression, and more averse to small talk, and reads far more history than I do. But she is an excellent roommate and an excellent friend. We use a sort of conversational shorthand with each other. There are things we would have to explain to other friends that we just understand—the crazy way our minds work, we go to each other for assurance that we are not in fact crazy because there is at least one other person in the world who thinks the same way we do.

I met Bev and Jordan on a ladies retreat for our church where I was giving a short testimony on Saturday night. It was during the winter when I was unemployed. I didn't want to be on the retreat, and I didn't want to meet them. I was just coming back from a conference in Tennessee; I was particularly exhausted; I felt like I had too many friends that I couldn't keep up with, that I was always disappointing people by not being able to get together with them, that I didn't have the energy for more friends—for more people who would call expecting things from me, forcing me to be social.

I went through several periods when I stopped returning calls. Talking on the phone is one of my least favorite activities, it drains my energy, and I didn't want to talk to anyone. So I might wait a week or two before calling back. Maybe there were times I didn't call back at all.

Bev and Jordan persisted. They taught me something about the nature of friendship, taught me to expect grace from my friends, that I didn't have to be perfect, that I could be struggling to figure out what to do with a nagging depression and they would still want to hang out with me.

We are so different. Jordan loves to talk. If she is not talking to someone she's with, she's likely on the phone—she calls people every day during her commute to and from work. She has more energy and concern for her friends than just about anyone I've ever known. Bev loves to shop. She has been known to buy a $150 shower curtain and declare it a bargain. She was born with expensive genes—she knows where to find the best quality kitchenware, the latest trend in Italian kitchen cabinets, the best places in Florence for leather bags. She could list cooking schools from various countries.

The three of them sat on the bed with me before I left, praying for me, earnest and thoughtful prayers. I know that I am important to them and they love me, and they've asked God to watch over me, and I'm so thankful. I need them. I know it now.

Then there are others more deep and longstanding—Suzanna, whom I've known for more than ten years, goes berry picking with me in the summers and used to go with me to crazy singles dances and to the beach, driving home singing every hymn we knew with all the old words. Now she lives in Maryland with her husband and three little ones. And Kristine, my writing friend, who first bonded with me over mutual heartbreak about seven years ago. Dear Catherine, who is so gracious and kind. And Leigh, my entrepreneurial business and movie friend. But these separate groups, these one-off friendships, sometimes feel like a random assortment of planets, an off-kilter solar system orbiting around me, and sometimes I fear that I cannot hold them together, and sometimes I feel alone in the middle.

❦

Margaret and I looked through all the pictures from my digital camera on her TV. I told her about Jack and asked, "What do you think it means that he said we will get together when I get home?" and she said, "Well, it means he wants to see you, I suppose."

Her thinking is very straightforward, and mine is all jumbled. And I would like answers, thank you very much.

I am interminably weak. I keep thinking that I will just stop thinking about him, but the frequency with which I think that alone is sign enough of how little success I'm having.

❦

We put together a merry party for Box Hill this morning—me and Margaret and her daughter Christine and her granddaughter Lucy. Unfortunately, in the tradition of Box Hill parties, it was not entirely a laughing affair. Box Hill is the setting for the picnic scene in *Emma*. Jane probably came to visit when she was staying with her cousins in Great Bookham. Today is cool with clouds, but you could still see enough of the view to admire it.

We walked around a bit—there are hiking trails enough to stay for a whole afternoon, but I was exhausted. Lucy wasn't feeling well, and Margaret was very sad about something going on in the family. So none of us was in the mood to be merry. We had coffee and then ate lunch at the picnic tables at the top—bacon and cheese muffins. (Everything is better when you eat it outside, especially on a day like this that feels almost like fall.) Lucy had part of a tuna sandwich with cucumber and then threw up, and I spent the ride home alternately sleeping and attempting to be sympathetic without being so sympathetic that I began to share her symptoms. (But really, the thought of cucumbers and tuna together is enough to make me sick.)

Emma's picnic at Box Hill, of course, is disastrous. Frank Churchill is there, secretly engaged to Jane Fairfax but flirting outrageously with Emma. Together Frank and Emma manage to be rude to nearly everyone, but the final straw comes when they are trying to find some kind of entertainment. Frank declares that Emma declares that everyone must provide something to entertain the group—"either one thing very clever...or two things moderately clever; or three things very dull indeed."[1]

Sweet, nervous Miss Bates replies, "I shall be sure to say three dull things as soon as ever I open my mouth, shan't I? Do not you think I shall?"[2]

Emma cuts her off: "Ah! ma'am, but there may be a difficulty. Pardon me, but you will be limited as to number—only three at once." Public humiliation ensues for poor Miss Bates.[3]

Others in the party are content to flatter Emma for her perfections, but dear Knightley (as the obnoxious Mrs. Elton calls him) simply cannot let this go. Walking Emma to her carriage, he scolds her the way only a dear friend can:

> Emma, I must once more speak to you as I have been used to
> do; a privilege rather endured than allowed, perhaps, but I must
> still use it. I cannot see you acting wrong without a remonstrance.
> How could you be so unfeeling to Miss Bates? How could you
> be so insolent in your wit to a woman of her character, age, and

situation? Emma, I had not thought it possible.... Her situation
should secure your compassion. It was badly done, indeed! You,
whom she had known from an infant, whom she had seen grow
up from a period when her notice was an honour—to have you
now, in thoughtless spirits and the pride of the moment, laugh
at her, humble her—and before her niece, too—and before others, many of whom (certainly *some*) would be entirely guided by
your treatment of her. This is not pleasant to you, Emma—and
it is very far from pleasant to me; but I must, I will—I will tell
you truths while I can.[4]

Emma has developed character faults natural to being spoiled and
the center of everyone's attention. She has grown accustomed to thinking very well of herself, but with this she is broken, and all of Mr.
Knightley's other gentle remonstrances—that she should be kinder to
Jane Fairfax, that she should not have led Mr. Elton on so, that she
should not be giving Harriet Smith grand ideas about herself—begin
to ring true. She has been pretty and well situated, only sometimes
kind, and not always good, and now she knows and feels it deeply.

Ultimately, this confrontation plays a large part in Emma's realizing her love for Mr. Knightley (that and Harriet's determination to
have him). She mends her ways, determines to be kinder, begins to
realize she is not entirely deserving of all the praise she receives. And
discovers that she loves him.

The pattern is repeated in almost all of Austen's books—not exactly,
but in some way each book is about a failing, the characters are confronted with their own faults, and for Austen the greatest good is being
willing to recognize these faults and change. I can't help but wonder—

and I imagine this is true—if she didn't consider herself guilty of each of the failings she created within her characters, particularly Emma's harsh wit and inability to genuinely love some of those in her circle. Jane wrote to Cassandra of neighborhood friends with a sarcasm that could be particularly harsh. "Mrs. Hall of Sherbourn was brought to bed yesterday of a dead child..." she writes, "oweing to a fright.—I suppose she happened unawares to look at her husband."[5] And later, "I respect Mrs. Chamberlayne for doing her hair well, but cannot feel a more tender sentiment.—Miss Langley is like any other short girl with a broad nose & wide mouth, fashionable dress, & exposed bosom."[6] All that to say, I think she understood Emma's failings.

Jane saw these progressions happening in the context of relationship. It was sisters, lovers, dear friends who would help work out the rough patches in one's character.

These are the kinds of relationships I crave and one of my highest priorities in a man, to find someone willing to lovingly correct me, willing like Mr. Knightley to say the difficult things without necessarily enjoying saying them. Someone both kind and strong. Perhaps this is one element of every good relationship; perhaps it is not as rare as I imagine.

I am afraid, though, that I will have to find someone with more emotional depth than Emma's dear Mr. Knightley.

Dom Nicholas loves *Emma*. He said it is about being truly elegant. He said there was a quote about Mrs. Elton being "as elegant as lace and pearls could make her."[7] I love that. Mrs. Elton, I'm sure, had horrible taste in lace and pearls anyway, so I imagine she was completely hopeless.

Eleven

The British Library

How horrible it is to have so many people killed!

— JANE AUSTEN IN A LETTER TO CASSANDRA

By London, my adventure had become mundane; I was growing weary of stalking Jane. I was determined not to be afraid, but the ride down the escalator to the Tube at Charing Cross station gave me plenty of time to consider how deep into the earth I was going, and how difficult it might be to get out, and how horrible it would be if something happened.

Margaret tried to talk me out of this, thinking that since terrorists walked on and blew up multiple trains during rush hour two weeks ago, perhaps the Tube should be avoided. She was also determined to go with me. "Now, if we get off here we can catch a double-decker bus. We would have to walk across the street, but it's not very far. And that would take us right to… Where is the library again? Do you know the address? Of course, we could just take a cab. It wouldn't cost that much, I suppose."

It's sweet really, her wanting to take care of me. She felt responsible for me, even though I am thirty-three. I was determined to talk her out of it though—not that my decision really came easily. Everyone said before I left, "At least it happened just before your trip. They never strike in the same place twice." And then there was Andrew at the monastery, his wonderful voice telling me to be careful, that there had been another incident. So I was fully aware that I could get on the Tube only to have the whole thing explode and be blown to bits or—perhaps worse—be stuck in a tunnel full of smoke with no way to get out, waiting for some kind of end or some kind of rescue, unsure which it would be. Still I thought it unlikely. I refused to be perpetually afraid. And Margaret, who is claustrophobic and hates the city anyway and would be bored to death by the things I'm seeing, stayed home where she will be much more comfortable.

A guy with a thick down coat (it's hardly that cold) and a backpack gets on, so in the name of self-preservation I get on a different car, holding my breath nearly the whole time, thinking how the world has gone awry.

⁂

The British Library sounds dull enough, but Jane's writing desk and a manuscript chapter from *Persuasion* are on display, so I thought I might as well stop by.

Now I can hardly walk straight, all tingly and in awe, as though my breath has been taken away. I thought perhaps I might throw up, like a silly little romantic heroine upon walking into a ballroom and seeing her long-lost love.

I went to the information desk, asked where the Austen material was, and began to think, *Of course, they have far more than just J. A. material.*

When I walked into the display room—the Sir John Ritblat Gallery—I began to get a sense of how much I had underestimated the library. I had to walk past the music case to get to the literature—I skipped the Beatles stuff and stumbled on to find original scores, quickly and greedily realizing that they were Beethoven's *Ninth,* Handel's *Messiah,* Bach's *Well-Tempered Clavier,* and something from Mozart.

To be so close—on the other side of thick glass, looking through dim light—to these manuscripts that they actually touched, that they wrote. I determined to stand there until I had them memorized.

Beethoven's is a huge thick book done by one of his copyists; it includes Beethoven's corrections, but I can't tell which notes are his. Bach's is a single sheet of music, and the notes themselves are musical, almost joyful—neat, full round notes with squiggly lines connecting them. They have *Messiah* open to the "Hallelujah Chorus," and Handel is gloriously messy. Jane said once, half-joking to Cassandra, "An artist cannot do anything slovenly."[1] But sometimes it's too difficult to be neat and create. Handel's writing is large and scrawled, with the words not entirely written out: "And he shall reign for ever and eve… Alleluia Alleluia." I suppose Jane would have known all these composers. Her great-great-uncle, the Duke of Chandos, was actually one of Handel's patrons.[2]

In the literature case is a copy of *Beowulf* from the eleventh century—the only surviving manuscript—individual disintegrating pages with a brown script I cannot read glued into a big book. There's romance literature from Italy, writing from Alexander Pope. Charlotte Brontë's notebook with *Jane Eyre*—tiny perfect writing with tons of space in between the lines, open to the part where Rochester proposes. Next to Brontë, Austen. Her small script with lines crossed through and words corrected looks like a mess compared to Brontë. Then there is Lewis Carroll, the original *Alice's Adventures Underground,* which he illustrated himself and later became *Alice in Wonderland.* An early edition of Dickens, a typewritten page of Virginia Woolf with her husband's notes.

In the middle of the room is a lease that Shakespeare may or may not have actually signed. A ship's log has an account of Nelson's death from a French musket shot on the deck of the *Victory.* Nelson actually thought very highly of Jane's brother Frank, who was then captain of the *Canopus.* Frank just missed the Battle of Trafalgar, where Nelson died. He regretted it all his life. He had been assigned to protect a convoy to Cartagena and turned back as soon as he got word of the enemy fleet leaving Cadiz, but by the time he got back everything was over.[3] Perhaps his life would have been completely different had he been there. He had survived battles enough—regular routs where he captured or destroyed multiple ships that should have completely overpowered him within shooting distance from cliff-side batteries[4]—but perhaps he would not have been so lucky at Trafalgar. As it was, he was safely and regrettably away, and Nelson was lost.

I felt as though I had walked into a sacred space, and everywhere I turned there was something new to inspire awe. I wondered about all of these people, the people whose work is here. Aside from genius, and a great gift, I think what they must have in common is a great energy for life, a not holding back. They kept going—whether it was art, or science, or music, or all of the above, they were determined to seek things out, to create. And to go in their given direction. (Had Jane attempted to write Bach's *Well-Tempered Clavier*—or even Brontë's *Jane Eyre*—she would have failed miserably. She knew what her realm was, what she called her "little bit (two Inches wide) of Ivory on which I work with so fine a Brush, as produces little effect after much labour."[5] I could feel their energy. Perhaps the gift inside them could not be silenced. Perhaps they could not help it. Madeleine L'Engle says you know you are a writer if you can't help but write, if you feel like you must.[6] I feel like I must. I want to obey that calling. I'm not a genius. I would be content simply to do some good work. It's possible to stifle things like this from laziness, or to choke them with fear or even misplaced humility. But when you can be brave, what a joy to have a chance to discover and create. That's how I felt wandering through all this greatness.

I found a speech written by Queen Elizabeth I on the subject of her proposed marriage. It is a mess—large writing, words and sentences crossed out, things written in the margins, sideways, so that the page is all filled up. And I turned around to see the actual Magna Carta. Unbelievable. I stared almost unseeing at a page from da Vinci's notebook until my mesmerized brain was absolutely full.

Then, as if to make everything else seem unimportant, I wandered over to King's Cross to have a look at Harry Potter's dear Platform 9¾.

Twelve

On Beauty

*Catherine hoped at least to pass uncensured through
the crowd. As for admiration, it was always very
welcome when it came, but she did not depend on it.*

—*NORTHANGER ABBEY*

Jane was not beautiful. I think this is one of the reasons I like her, or the idea of her. Actually, really, we don't know what she looked like. The only sure likeness we have of her face is a little pencil and watercolor drawing her sister did that looks like just the work of an afternoon and that no one thought looked especially like her at the time. The proportions seem off—the shoulders slope, the eyes and mouth and shape of the head and neck are not quite right—yet nearly every image we have of her has been adapted somehow from this. They probably never imagined it would make it outside their little family circle. And now it sits in a little case in the National Portrait Gallery in London, the light going off and on from time to time to protect it. It is softer and fainter than I imagined it would be.

Jane's neighbors thought she was "a very pretty girl,"[1] but her niece Anna, who grew to be very close to her aunt in spite of their seventeen years difference, presents a slightly harsher view. She talks of her "Figure tall & slight...her quick firm step," her "clear & healthy" complexion, "the fine naturally curling hair, neither light nor dark; the bright hazel eyes to match, & the rather small but well shaped nose." Which all sounds very nice. Then Anna adds: "One hardly understands how with all these advantages she could yet fail of being a decidedly handsome woman."[2]

I've often felt that way myself—there are parts that should add up to a good-looking whole but don't entirely. Tall and thin, with lovely eyes, a decent complexion (not as much of that smooth tan as I would like to have gotten from my Norwegian forebears, but still decent), thickish brown hair that looks good when I do something with it, although that's not very often, and cheeks that are "a little too full,"[3] which is how another family acquaintance described Jane. My ears are definitely crooked, and there are moments when I look in the mirror and think the jowls are beginning. I've often thought that if there is beauty here, it is with a kind of weirdness underlying it—like the disproportions of Cassandra's sketch—that throws everything off.

This is one difference between my brother and me—he seems entirely assured of his own good looks, and I am always questioning mine. I think this must be one of the thousands of settings God tweaks when we are being made—the tendency to confidence or to doubt. On most anything, my brother's bent is to be completely sure of himself; mine is to question.

Our world prizes physical beauty like nothing else. As a woman, to attain perfection—that antithetical starved yet voluptuous look that is the current American fashion—is the highest good. Other normal sorts of bodies—other normal sorts of people—are not as valuable. And you can tell yourself hundreds of times that this is all ridiculous, which it is, but it creates a gnawing self-doubt that is ready to welcome you anytime you start to feel weird.

We all have our insecurities. Mine, aside from my amazing disappearing chin, is my stomach, which I would actually prefer to disappear entirely. My friends think it's ridiculous. I try to tell them that I am actually a fat little skinny girl, and they don't believe me (until one of them saw me in a bathing suit and said, "I can see why you say that.") Actually, I have been surreptitiously watching at Pilates classes and such, and I'm beginning to think that "fat little skinny girl" is an entirely normal body type. There are thousands of us, skinny girls that look ridiculous in bikinis.

The thing is, it's easy to hide this particular fault with a good outfit, a series of carefully constructed optical illusions. But it is still there, in my mind, this weird little body, my skinny little frame with the stomach of a much larger woman, and I know it even when other people don't.

I don't believe in plastic surgery. For one thing, I think it's far easier to learn to be content with your body than to have someone knock you out, cut you open, and suck things out or stuff foreign objects inside you. Maybe I've got that wrong. Maybe surgery really is easier than contentment. But I think contentment is healthier and more admirable and in some way much more attractive. So I'm trying not to be ridiculous, trying to be content with a little beauty, choosing to believe that my stomach looks big only because the rest of me is so very small.

My sister-in-law, who is wise and witty, tells me that women are supposed to have stomachs. Jane probably had a stomach and couldn't have cared. But then they were (and I think the British still are) much more satisfied with normal sorts of bodies than we are. I don't think Jane would have wanted to be the most beautiful person in the room. I imagine she was incredibly content with her own little blend of beauty and intelligence and wit.

She does not give her characters detailed physical descriptions. Our introduction to Lizzy is simply that "she is not half so handsome as Jane."[4] In the first sentence of *Emma,* we learn that she is "handsome, clever, and rich."[5] Enough to get an instant impression and all we need to know for the moment, but details of hair or face or clothes are clearly unimportant. More carefully drawn is *Persuasion*'s Anne Elliot, who "had been a very pretty girl, but her bloom had vanished early." In spite of her "delicate features and mild dark eyes," she is "faded and thin."[6] With just a few words we know what Anne was like. Jane tells us little but everything we need. She didn't labor over this. We get to know her characters mostly through what they say, their friendships, their place in society, the choices they make.

Characters actually—as in moral character, not fictional creations— are described with much more detail in Austen's writing than faces ever are. Long before we know of Elinor's "remarkably pretty figure"[7] and that "there was a life, a spirit, an eagerness"[8] in Marianne's eyes, we learn of Elinor's "strength of understanding and coolness of judgment" and that Marianne is "everything but prudent." She has resolved never to learn to govern her emotions and is "sensible and clever, but eager in everything; her sorrows, her joys, could have no moderation."[9]

We can't fully know our own character. I think this is one of our greatest weaknesses—something Jane certainly understood. Like our physical appearances, some of us have no doubt of being handsome when in fact we are plain; some who are beautiful think they are ugly.

I have no luck making myself out. I'm perversely prone to err on both sides—at once to think myself incredibly good and to be plunged into despair for never having a completely unselfish feeling, for not being genuinely loving, to have all my faults overwhelm me at once. We are human; we have blind spots. There are egregious flaws of which we are completely unaware. And mostly our friends and family are loathe to say anything about them. I wonder if we really even want them to. It's possible to live all our lives without understanding who we really are, what we are really like.

I am a strange mixture of incredible inner strength and great insecurity, of a desire to laugh and an intense and often overly serious view of the world, of occasional bravery and great, awkward shyness. As a child I learned to be sweet, which perhaps is good in a child, but it's something that developed into an act. I learned to appear nice, to say and do the right thing. I was too afraid of voicing my own opinion, of being real. I could analyze this in detail; multiple reasons and multiple and complex streams of thought and behavior converge here. But as Jane would say, it was affected behavior. As the apostle Paul would say, I have often been "a clanging cymbal" (1 Corinthians 13:1), worthless without genuine love.

What I am today I would guess is something like my physical appearance—a fat-little-skinny-girl kind of soul that looks more than acceptable in most lights, but doesn't tolerate minute inspection. (And if God were to pull back the covers to show me myself in the stark light of absolute Truth, I'm sure I would be overwhelmed with hopelessness. Praise God he does not let us see ourselves as we truly are, at least not all at once.) I hope that my friends and family—and gentle proddings from God—will move me in the right direction, that I will, in spite of my hopeless pride, be open to some kind of reproof, that I'll be able to discern which corrections to heed and what of my own self-condemnation is completely unnecessary. I'm tired of being human, with all the necessary imperfections that implies. If nothing else, I've learned to laugh at my own occasional ridiculousness, which gives me hope.

❧

One of my favorite characters in Jane's life is her charming and favorite brother, Henry—tall, good-looking Henry, who loved everything he did and simultaneously always wanted to be doing something else, who spent time in the militia and contemplated importing wine from France and was part owner of a bank until it went bankrupt. He finally ended up, enthusiastic as always, in the church, disappointed that the bishop who ordained him had no desire to read the New Testament text in the original Greek.

You can't tell the story of Henry without talking about Eliza, the Austens' beautiful, romantic French cousin, whom he eventually married. Eliza was actually born in India, where her mother had successfully gone in search of a husband. But she spent some of her growing-up years in France, married a French army officer who liked to be known as a count—but doesn't seem to have actually been a count[10]—and visited Versailles, where she adored the "Feathers, ribbon & diamonds" in Marie Antoinette's [May 16, 1780] hair and found her ungloved hands "without exception the whitest & most beautiful I ever beheld."[11]

You can imagine the stories she told when she came back to visit the Austens in their country rectory, speaking French like a native and being generally flirtatious. Unfortunately, the dear count (it's unclear how much Eliza really loved him) lost his life to the guillotine in the Revolution (February 1794).[12] Eliza returned to England, and it took a great deal of persuasion for Henry, ten years her junior, to talk her out of the charms of being single and able to flirt with every man in the room.[13] James had been interested as well, but Henry won, and James went on to Mary Lloyd, who could never really love Eliza knowing that James had wanted her once.

Eliza died young of what may have been breast cancer, and Henry, who did not have "a Mind for affliction"[14] and was not of a disposition to wallow in grief, went back to being the charming man-about-town, even dancing at the royal ball at Burlington House in 1814 celebrating peace with France, where the Prince Regent, the Czar of Russia, and the King of Prussia were in attendance. "Oh! what a Henry," Jane said.[15]

Henry was the one who couldn't bear for Jane's authorship to remain a secret. It seems that whenever the books were mentioned— and they were popular even then—he couldn't help but mention, against her wishes, that his sister was the author. He handled all of her business negotiations with publishers.

He lived here in Covent Garden for a while (he was always moving), but my hopes for the place have all been dashed. There's too much junk and higher-end chain stores. I sit in a wine bar with my backpack and notebook, drinking bubbly water, thinking one should probably never bring a backpack into a wine bar. A couple guys look my way, and as always, I can't determine if they're meditating on my beauty or my overall strangeness.

Henry reminds me of my own brother. When he walks into a roomful of people he doesn't know, he is sure to win them over. As a child, I thought his gregariousness was strength, my own shyness weakness.

He told me a few years ago that this was just the particular way his own insecurities worked themselves out. But there's something there—an ease and self-assurance—that I've always wanted desperately, at least as soon as I realized they were missing. I'm sure Henry had them as well. I think that is so much of what makes someone good-looking to us—not physical beauty, but a confidence and force of personality that often has nothing to do with looks.

⁂

I went to a candlelight concert in the church of St. Martin-in-the-Fields—Bach and Handel with a chamber orchestra, gorgeous and comforting. Music like that fills me up and holds on to me, reassuring me.

And then I came home to Margaret and the news, which I cannot watch anymore. It is mostly about terrorism, but the last several nights they've been covering the famine in Niger, following one small boy. I don't know how old he is, maybe eighteen months, but he lies on the ground with a head that looks far too big for his tiny body. His stomach is distended; his face is crusty. There are flies. He's dying, and they are there to film it.

I am sick of seeing death and being unable to do anything about it. I can't bear to just send my twenty dollars to some massive aid organization. I want to do something meaningful.

"They took turns in those days, you know," Dom Nicholas had said. We were having coffee—Anselm, Susan, Nicholas, and I before Susan and I headed out to Chawton. He was talking about how people used to take care of one another in Austen's day, how they made soup for the poor. "Everyone knew when it was their turn, when it was their week. You see, they understood their responsibility. They took care of each other. And if you were going to skimp, you didn't put meat in the soup, but the Austens always used meat. They took their responsibility seriously."

I know Jane made shirts for the poor, people she knew who lived in Steventon. I know she bought them things they needed—shifts and stockings and shawls. I feel both isolated from poverty—I do not know what my neighbors need or if they need anything—and surrounded by it because now we know about all the hunger and death in the world, and everyone is my neighbor.

I want to make soup.

Thirteen

An *A* Road in Kent

Is there a felicity in the world superior to this?

—MARIANNE, *SENSE AND SENSIBILITY*

Do you know the scene in the old movie *It Happened One Night* where a glamorous Claudette Colbert shows a little leg for the sake of stopping traffic since Clark Gable is having no luck hitchhiking? If you can imagine a situation almost entirely the opposite, you'll have a pretty good idea of my predicament this afternoon. I was standing on the narrow shoulder of an A road in Kent (whoever knew that A roads are the busiest roads in the countryside?), drenched from rain, my hair in strings around my face, any trace of makeup gone, my hiking shoes soaked, my pants wet four inches deep. Only I don't know how to hitchhike the cool way, so I looked like a soaked crazy woman having an incredibly bad hair day sticking out my thumb in the manner of a librarian and occasionally trying to wave cars down. No one stopped.

One of my most frequent prayers of late is that I will just not be an idiot. And I don't mean the socially awkward, always saying the wrong things at the wrong time kind of idiot, though perhaps I should pray for that more as I have some talent in that area. I mean the kind of proud, ridiculous idiot who thinks highest of herself and as a result whose life adds up to very little in the end. But this was idiocy of a whole other kind. I often question God's direct involvement in my life as a result of prayer, but I begged him with everything in me to please do something to get me off the side of that A road in Kent.

It's been an ugly day, both for me and the weather. I wore my green cropped sweatpants and dark red tank, which would have been okay, except that I had to wear my hiking shoes, which threw the whole outfit off, and then it was so cold that I had to put on my red fleece, which clashed with everything, and it was raining off and on, so I kept putting on and taking off my rain jacket, which clashed with the fleece. I had planned to try Winchester today, but they were doing work on the tracks in that direction this morning. Instead, Margaret drove me to the Bromley station, and I was able to get a train directly to Canterbury.

The town center is small, the streets narrow. The sky was gray and spitting wet. I found my way from the train station to the cathedral, just after the morning service had started. To me it felt oppressive and lifeless—maybe because it was so gray and cold—and the sermon, from the little attention I had for it, seemed to be rubbish, full of weak analogies with little strength and conviction.

By 1:00 I was choking on a dry ham omelet in a great little café above the tourist center, and at 1:25 I caught the train to Chilham from the West train station on the other side of town. The lady at the tourist center had never heard of Godmersham. *Very bad beginning,* I thought. Then when she did look up the bus schedule, she said the buses didn't run on Sunday, so I should take the train to Chilham and get a cab from there, which would be much cheaper.

I sat in the café drinking my watered-down instant decaf, feeling like an ugly, conspicuous, backpack-toting tourist. I felt like I couldn't do anything right and had far too many un-chic accoutrements. I wondered if I should even try to find Godmersham, what kind of challenges I would find, if it would even be worth the effort. So I made a conscious decision to choose adventure. And that is when the fun began.

Chilham is the smallest train station I have seen yet. There were no cabs, not even a shack, no phone numbers posted on a sign anywhere. Everyone who got off the train with me disappeared. I started to walk in what seemed like the direction of town. I passed a tea shop and thought perhaps I should stop there to call a cab, but just beyond it was a signpost that said Godmersham. I remembered that Chilham was mentioned in my walking guidebook, so I looked it up there at the side of the road and found it was only two or three miles, but the writer recommended a back way through fields, and I couldn't figure that out. Better to stick to the road. It had stopped raining, although it was spitting a little. There was even a marked walking path beside the road, so I set out. What's two or three miles on a walking path by a country road in spitting rain to reach a village no one has ever heard of? I could hear Marianne from the pages of *Sense and Sensibility* saying, "It's not going to rain." And anyway, it's nothing I mind at all.

The walking trail quickly veered off to the left, and I decided to follow the road instead. It started to rain again, harder, until it was raining so hard it seemed to be coming straight through my Gore-Tex jacket, under which I was sweating from the exertion. I tried to keep my hood up to keep my head dry, but it cut off my vision and eventually just annoyed me, so I took it down and let my head get soaked. The shoulder was gradually disappearing.

Fifteen minutes in, I knew it was a mistake. But I thought, *How much farther can it be?* Fifteen more minutes and the shoulder was completely gone, so I was walking in the road and jumping up on the bank between trees when I heard cars coming. Every car that went by—and they were going very fast—splashed me with water. The road curved so much that I thought how easy it would be for a car to whip around a corner and hit me dead-on. I was officially terrified. But now I was thirty minutes into the walk, and I know I can easily walk a mile in fifteen minutes, so I thought it really couldn't be that much farther.

I slipped on the wet grass and landed on nettles of some kind. All I could think was, *What if I had slipped into the road?* I passed a simple, expensive-looking house with handcrafted bronze gates. Feeling incredibly foolish, I rang the intercom, but the phone on the other end just rang and rang and no one picked up.

So I made it to a little clearing and stuck out my thumb and prayed very, very hard. A cabby went by without stopping. Loads of people alone or with families, completely immune to my crazy, drenched, desperate hand waving. And then the best cabby, William, went by in one direction, saw my pitiful thumb, turned around, and came back. Cue the trumpet voluntary. God saved me from my own stupidity.

"You're awfully wet," William said. He drove me to Godmersham, first to the church and then to the big house, turned off his meter and sat and waited for me for twenty minutes while I walked through the fields to see the house. He wasn't creepy at all, which a girl might worry about in this situation. He had short dark hair, bright blue eyes, and a solid build. Nothing about him was messy.

Godmersham was glorious. It had stopped raining, and I walked into the fields under a heavy gray sky. You can't get into the house (at least I couldn't find contact information for anyone), which is now a professional school of some kind. So I took the walking path through the sheep pasture, next to the cows, and up a hill into a cornfield to look down on everything. It's simple and grand, gorgeous red brick, classical lines with two rows of windows and two wings on either end and maybe more in the back. The house sits in the valley of the Stour, broad hills rising behind and in front of it. When Jane came to visit, they made a point of hiking (or walking as they called it) in the afternoons. I wish I had hours to explore.

Jane and Cassandra spent a great deal of time here, often separately, helping with household duties around the birth of the latest child. There were eleven children before Elizabeth died at thirty-five.[1] Cassandra seems to have been Elizabeth's favorite. No doubt Cassandra was more compliant, Jane's wit more disconcerting. Jane's niece Anna said, "A little talent went a long way with the Goodneston Bridgeses [Elizabeth's family] of that period; & *much* must have gone a long way too far."[2] And Jane, who loved to laugh at everyone, herself included, no doubt found material enough at Godmersham.

I got back in the cab and William said, "You're still awfully wet," and drove me all the way back to Canterbury. We had a little bond going, William and I. When he found out about the Austen connection, he wanted to take me out to Goodnestone as well (which was the Bridges' home, Edward's in-laws), but I couldn't afford another adventure. It felt wrong somehow though to just say good-bye to him there in the tourist district of Canterbury, feeling like he had saved my life.

At 5:09 p.m. in Faversham, on the train back, the sun came out. My feet were still soaked.

Margaret has made me promise never to hitchhike again. She laughed at me, of course (which I have no problem with because I am laughing at myself anyway), and has refused my help with dinner, sitting me on the couch with tea and biscuits while she makes quiche. I will miss her tomorrow when I leave. The view of Godmersham from the fields was worth everything. And I am full of quick-hearted joy, with a much more palpable sense of the hand of God in my life, which perhaps sounds ridiculous in light of the day's events, but I'm thankful most of all that my own stupidity does not negate his goodness.

PART 3

*In which I stumble
upon deeper meanings of grace.*

Fourteen

Winchester: A Patient Descent

She was the sun of my life,
the gilder of every pleasure, the soother of
every sorrow, I had not a thought concealed from her,
& it is as if I had lost a part of myself.

—CASSANDRA AUSTEN, AFTER JANE'S DEATH

Jane came to Winchester to die. I think she knew that. She drew up her will in late April 1817 without telling any of her family. By the end of May, she and Cassandra were here in a house at 8 College Street behind some windy roads from the cathedral so Jane could be treated by the surgeon Mr. Lyford.[1] He told Jane that he would cure her but soon privately told family members that there was no hope. In June everyone thought she was dying, but she rallied again and lasted until mid-July. Her sister, Cassandra, was there, and her sister-in-law Mary. Her brothers had been visiting, all but Frank, whose seventh child was just three months old and who may have agreed to stay home to keep their mother company.[2]

At the end, Cassandra asked if Jane wanted anything, and she told her "she wanted nothing but death" and said, "God grant me patience, Pray for me Oh Pray for me."[3]

Early the next morning, she was gone.

Nearly everyone in Jane's family lived into their seventies or eight-ies. Her mother, who regularly suffered from all kinds of illnesses, like a "gouty swelling & sensation," bile, "heat in her throat," "an Asthma, a Dropsy, Water in her Chest & a Liver Disorder"[4] would outlive her by ten years, her sister by nearly thirty. James died shortly after Jane, but Frank and Charles were both commanding ships in their seventies. Charles died at seventy-three of cholera in Burma, serving as rear admi-ral.[5] Frank lived to the ripe old age of ninety-one.[6] Edward lived to be eighty-five, and dear Henry almost as long.[7] In a world where sickness and death were so much more readily expected, the Austens were remarkably healthy. Jane was just forty-one.

She had been sick for a year and a half.[8] It was a strange illness no one understood at the time. It made her tired so that she often had to lie down. Her back hurt sometimes, and her skin went blotchy—black and white. She had fevers and difficulty sleeping and enough gastro-intestinal problems to make her believe that bile—that general nineteenth-century malady supposed to be responsible for so much illness—was the cause of the whole thing. At the end, she would be stuck on a sofa during the days and brag of being able to get up from time to time and move from room to room. Some suggest this was cancer, but most now believe it was Addison's disease, which had yet to be named. With Addison's, the adrenal glands go askew, and the body's fine balance is disturbed.

Jane was always hopeful that it was going away. There were periods when she couldn't take her regular walks so she used a donkey cart to get out or even rode the donkey itself, which she sometimes found eas-ier. She was always trying to get better, always expecting that she was getting better. She wrote to her niece Caroline, "*I* feel myself getting stronger than I was half a year ago, & can so perfectly well walk to Alton, *or* back again, without the slightest fatigue that I hope to be able to do both when Summer comes."[9] And to Fanny, "Sickness is a dangerous Indulgence at my time of Life."[10] Some days she rested on a group of three chairs in a row, never taking the couch for fear that her mom might need to lie down there and would never use it if she thought Jane might need it.

She finished writing *Persuasion* as the fog was setting in (not that there is any symptom of this fog in her writing), then started *Sanditon* and had to put it aside fairly quickly.

Her illness got worse with stress, and there was stress during this period in the Austen family. Edward had been dealing with a lawsuit that threatened all of his Hampshire properties, including Chawton and Steventon.[11] Charles, whose wife and new baby had died a couple of years earlier, ran the naval ship he was commanding aground along the Turkish coast.[12] It was all proved not to be his fault, but he would have had to go through a court-martial, and it was a black mark against his name. Henry's banking business failed, which cost the family dearly.[13] Then Uncle Leigh-Perrot, Mrs. Austen's wealthy brother, died and left them nothing immediately, instead giving everything to his wife. The Austens had reason to hope for something from his will and were greatly disheartened—and if that sounds moneygrubbing, at that period of time, families were largely dependent on one another, and Leigh-Perrot was immensely wealthy compared to the Austens.[14] So Jane would get worse, and then she would recover and believe she was getting better, but it would never actually go away—only return again and again with a stealthy ferocity.

I think Jane had always been preparing for this moment. Reading her letters, there is an awareness and remembrance of what would be next. She was conscious of that other world that is a focus of Christianity. This life, however good or bad, was thought of as preparation for the next. In one of her letters to her brother Frank—Frank who was known as the devout sailor, the one "who knelt in church"[15]—she wrote of her growing fame, "what a trifle it is in all its Bearings, to the really important points of one's existence even in this World!"[16] (Actually, what Jane was concerned about was Henry's letting out her secret career as a writer.)

Jane, with humility that prevailed in spite of her sharp wit and sometimes sharp tongue, was not sure she was entirely prepared for death. In one of her last letters, sent when Jane still believed she was recovering, she tells her friend Anne Sharp, "the Providence of God has restored me—& may I be more fit to appear before him when I *am* summoned, than I should have been now!"[17] I can only imagine what she felt, to be so sick so young, to have hope because of the grace of God and yet feel like more could have been done, more years were wanted.

The Austens—particularly Cassandra—seem to have stifled their grief a bit in light of their great Christian hope of another world, of Jane being acceptable to God, and even of someday being together again. They were both devastated and stalwart, with tangible hope.

⁂

I am afraid it looked like I was moving into the cathedral for a while. I decided to stop through on my way to Lyme so I had to drag my suitcase and backpack with me the whole way; because of all the terrorism, the tourist office will no longer hold on to them. So I rolled the whole unbalanced mess through the line, in front of the desk where they plead for a donation, up to the center of the nave, out the side door up the steps and through the turnstile into the bathroom, back in through the exit up the nave and over to the side aisle to look for Austen's memorial, up the steps at the back of the church to try to see the choir loft and chapels. My luggage sat beside me as reverently as possible.

The whole town felt better and more real than Canterbury. The brick streets are wider; there is still commerce but less schmaltz. They seem to be stores that real people use. You can walk through the whole center of town, which is blocked off to traffic. There were people out doing business, and not just hordes of tourists (sneers the girl dragging her suitcase behind her).

I loved the cathedral, in spite of the noise and crowds of school-children, not all of whom had intelligent, good-looking masters keep-ing them in line. ("*Scuze, scuze,*" I was interrupted by a group of Italian junior-high kids in the middle of my reverie in front of Jane's memorial. They will not remember what it was when they get home and look at the pictures.) And I know this is a building Jane loved. It's so much like Canterbury that I don't know how they could feel so materially differ-ent, but Winchester felt open and welcoming; Canterbury felt heavy and dark and oppressive. Huge green spaces around the cathedral were filled with groups of teenagers hanging out, talking, and smoking.

My favorite is the back window, a jumble of colors and patterns. The panes, as most, had portrayed various biblical stories, but they were ruined by the parliamentary forces of William Waller during the Civil War. Waller's troops entered the church during a morning service—some on horseback, with noise and drums and chaos, and decided to use the window for target practice. The local story is that when the towns-people heard, they rushed in and gathered up all the pieces. Twenty years later, the original pieces of glass were put back in however they could get them to fit, so now it is an entire wall of comforting mess.

They say in the early years after Jane's death people would come to see her grave, and the verger had no idea why they were looking for the grave of this country girl. She was buried here almost a week after she died with the epitaph Henry wrote for her tomb:

> The benevolence of her heart,
> the sweetness of her temper, and
> the extraordinary endowments of her mind
> obtained the regard of all who knew her, and
> the warmest love of her intimate connections.
> Their grief is in proportion to their affection
> they know their loss to be irreparable,
> but in their deepest affliction they are consoled
> by a firm though humble hope that her charity,
> devotion, faith and purity, have rendered
> her soul acceptable in the sight of her
> REDEEMER.

"They know their loss to be irreparable." I love that line. Her nieces and nephews said that they went back to the Chawton Cottage after they had grown up a bit, after Jane was gone and when Cassandra was getting older. They found it had none of the charm they remembered.

Henry, Edward, Frank, and Jane's nephew James Edward carried the coffin. Women did not go to funerals then, for fear of their emotions, so Cassandra could only watch the procession carry her sister, "the sun of [her] life," until they went down the street and around the corner and she "had lost her forever."[18]

Jane's death makes me think of my Aunt Ginny. She was lovely. I mean not in the traditional beautiful person sense, but she was a lovely person. Her face and hair sort of reminded me of a throwback to the forties, maybe because her hair never really changed from when she got married in the middle of World War II just as her fiancé was about to ship off—short curls, not entirely natural, carefully put in place. She let me and my sister curl it once when we were staying in a condo on Kauai and she was out of town for her regular hair appointment. She sat there in a chair in front of the mirror, and we laughed and tried to figure out how to do an old person's hair. That was the trip where the police came one night and told us to quiet down because we were being too loud playing spoons and singing old country music. I was fifteen then; Ginny was in her early sixties and already had cancer. I didn't think too much about it, I guess, except that you had to expect stuff like that when you got old.

And when I was seventeen and she, in tears, put her mother's—my grandmother's—pearls around my neck, passing them on to the next generation (I think she must have known too that she was dying, although that would take another year and a half), I felt young and beautiful and deserving, not able to comprehend the greatness, the significance of the gift.

Back then women were still allowed to get old. Ginny's hair had turned gray, her hips were a little wide, her chest a little flat. She was eighteen years older than my mom, so more like a grandmother to me than an aunt. Her eyes danced whenever we came to visit, and she was the one I took my first steps to on my first birthday.

She and Uncle Steve went on cruises and sent us postcards from places like St. Thomas and St. Lucia, and every Valentine's Day without fail she sent a heart-shaped box of Russell Stover candy.

My mom went to stay with Ginny when she was dying since Steve had passed on years before. Her colon cancer had spread, had eaten through her body so that there was a hole to the outside. She was in tremendous pain. Now I realize that she was young, my parents' age now, and that she could still be here if they had caught the cancer sooner or if they had different treatments.

I was a sophomore in college. My mother called and said there would only be a very small memorial service, that I shouldn't come. Reluctantly I let her persuade me. I regretted it even then. So Ginny was cremated, her possessions gone through, the house with the lovely hardwood floors sold. A small group of friends gathered to remember her, and I cried myself to sleep in a metal bunk bed in a sterile dorm room in gray, rainy Ohio.

I can only imagine how Cassandra felt watching Jane's coffin proceed from the house on College Street toward the cathedral, through the ancient Kingsgate Arch, where she wouldn't be able to watch any further.

⚜

The first time I wanted to die I was driving by Chestnut Grove Cemetery off Drainesville Road, which I drive by all the time. I was sick then—I mean, I hadn't fully recovered from that mono-like virus, so I was exhausted all the time and working full time and trying to be a writer (I think I was finishing my first book) and training on the weekends for the upcoming week-long backpacking trip to Montana. More than anything else I wanted rest, and in that moment death seemed attractive, like the only way to stop doing and just rest, for ages and ages. Strangely, there was nothing depressing about it. I just envied the silence and stillness of the dead.

Then when I was flying home from my grandfather's funeral—irascible old Granddaddy Bob, who was mean with a tinge of sweetness and sometimes the other way around ("Do you know why you aren't married, Lori?" he said once. "It's because you're too religious.")—it hit me that death is our destination, which I had always known but had never really believed or maybe had never really believed for myself. This time I felt it with a kind of surety, like death is the main point. Bob was gone, and everyone else who had ever lived before me was gone, and all of us on the plane, all of us living, will someday be gone, and waves of people after us will all be heading for death. There is this great destination no one will escape, as if life were a churning assembly line sending us all on to death and dying. "A patient willing descent into the grass,"[19] Wendell Berry more graciously calls it. In that moment, whatever comes after this seemed to be the main point.

I was tired then—I still am—so maybe my thinking was slightly off. Since then I have turned the tables a bit and seen that in the face of the constant presence of death, there is irrepressible Life. But that realization never really left me.

Jack and I talked about heaven one night, sitting with Spencer on the Wycliffe back lawn. I don't know entirely what to make of the idea of heaven, but I do believe I'll see Jesus (which sounds terribly cheesy somehow) and that all the bad stuff in me will be gone so that in that moment I will finally have a right perspective of myself, that standing there I will be known, truly, and be able to worship, truly, without my muck and tainted heart getting in the way. The pride will be gone, and I will finally be true and put right again.

Anyway, Jack and I were talking with Spencer about how if heaven is this eternal hymn sing, then, please, just send me to hell (only writing that feels very sacrilegious). And how could we think that the God who gave us Bach and physics and the entire world of the oceans with their tiny tidal pools and extravagant creature-filled depths could have something boring planned? Why is it we suspect God of giving us less in the next world than he's given us in this?

All the same, I'm not really comfortable with the idea of death. I try to be, but I'm not.

This is what keeps me up at night, the mystery of what happens in that dying moment and my fear of God. Actually I think I am not that spiritual, and my much greater fear is simply the unknown. I am the girl, after all, who didn't go to the school cafeteria for an entire year because I wasn't entirely sure how it worked. I sat there with my nerdy brown bag, wanting tater tots and wondering what it looked like behind the wall in the kitchen. So contemplating a shift from here to eternity is a stretch for me. But I have "a firm though humble hope"[20] that in the face of my Redeemer, all will be well, and all will be well, and all manner of things shall be well.

Fifteen

Lyme: the Comforting Ocean

A little sea-bathing would set me up forever.

—MRS. BENNET, *PRIDE AND PREJUDICE*

For Jane's sake I'm sitting on a bench overlooking the beach in the cold gray mist, trying to love Lyme but not being very successful. I didn't expect this when the bus tipped over the edge of the hill and down into town last night. Suddenly we were out from beneath the overgrowth, the tiny roads that seemed to be carved into the edge of the cliff, running down the main street. Suddenly there was the comforting ocean, the quaint town with bright buildings and little stores. I expected to love it.

But my room was dirty and smelly, with white lacquered furniture from the seventies and only big enough for a twin bed, small walkway, dresser, desk, and sink lining the opposite wall. The sink and shower were growing black mold. The fabric headboard had a dark outline where people rubbed their dirty heads against it. I'm sure the carpet was filthy, but the colors were so dark that you couldn't see the dirt. The more I thought about that, the more I obsessively dropped things—my hairbrush, my socks, my pajamas. My room was right over the pub, so it reeked of frying oil from the fish and chips; I couldn't sleep for fear that I would touch something.

Now I'm looking at the beaches, which are mostly pebbles, big enough so you wouldn't want to walk on them barefoot. Big cement steps—two or three feet high—go straight into the water on one side of the beach just down the street from my hotel, so I sat there for a while today just looking at the gray water, wrapped up in my fleece, ignoring the spitting rain. Mostly it was picnickers on the beach—families with children, a father spending the day with his son, a beautiful little girl whose parents and grandparents could give her none of the attention she craved because they were too consumed with the baby and the dog.

I've walked down to the Cobb twice. Last night I couldn't help it; I couldn't be in Lyme and not try to find the Cobb and Granny's Teeth—the steps where Louisa Musgrove in *Persuasion* jumps into Captain Wentworth's arms, only he tells her not to jump—he thinks it's too high and too hard—and she does anyway and winds up unconscious on the Cobb. I bought some fudge, which turned out to be not so good and then got ice cream from a small store, from a guy who was leering at his teenage customers and had his hands all over the cone.

I walked back down today, past the ice-cream shops and candy stores, by stands for jacket potatoes and lovely seafood restaurants. There are children crabbing in the harbor and one brave and very white English guy in a Speedo wading into the water.

Jane writes so warmly of Lyme in *Persuasion:* "the remarkable situation of the town, the principal street almost hurrying into the water, the walk to the Cobb, skirting round the pleasant little bay...with the very beautiful line of cliffs stretching out to the east of town."[1] And then of everything else around here:

> "A very strange stranger it must be, who does not see charms in the immediate environs of Lyme, to make him wish to know it better. The scenes in its neighbourhood, Charmouth, with its high grounds and extensive sweeps of country, and still more, its sweet, retired bay, backed by dark cliffs, where fragments of low rock among the sands make it the happiest spot for watching the flow of the tide, for sitting in unwearied contemplation; the wooded varieties of the cheerful village of Up Lyme; and, above all, Pinny, with its green chasms between romantic rocks…these places must be visited, and visited again to make the worth of Lyme understood."[2]

I want to see Up Lyme and Pinny and Charmouth, to see the "green chasms between romantic rocks" and sit "in unwearied contemplation," but I'm too tired to hike the cliffs, so tired I don't even much care. I would like to have come in November, like Anne, when it is quieter, with a party of friends. Jane vacationed here with her parents and sister and Henry and Eliza.[3] I'm sure that's where her enthusiasm comes from, the fun they had exploring together.

The beach is the backdrop of so many of my best memories. Not active memories, mostly just sitting-and-being memories, soaking in the sun and sitting in a chair by the tip of the waves, reading all the way to the end of C. S. Lewis's dramatic retelling of the Cupid and Psyche myth in *Till We Have Faces,* wrapped in a towel against the cool clouds and intermittent sun, and a thousand other books. Walking into the quiet evening blue hour when everything glows and softens, as if watching the edge of the world get tucked in for the night. There is something about that hour at the beach—the softness and stillness and noise—that fills me with comfort and reminds me of what is holy. Then watching the tops of my feet turn brown and feeling the tightness and aliveness of a slight burn, tasting the salt in the air, smelling fish—dead and alive— watching the sea oats on the dunes, feeling the freedom and terror of wearing an acceptable kind of nearly nothing and just slipping on shorts and a T-shirt until the late, late afternoon. I love it in all its seasons, but I suppose more in the warm sun than in the cold, gray rain.

My parents have a place in Cape Hatteras, North Carolina—a little strip of an island sticking out into the Atlantic. It is sort of a down-home southern beach. There are big dunes, campgrounds, and restaurants that seem to change every season. If you need groceries, you can go to Joe Bob's or the gas station. As a child, vacation meant Hawaii or camp- ing under the pines at Myrtle Beach, where we went paddle boating in a lake with crocodiles, or the wide, wet slabs of Corpus Christi, where we hunted sand dollars in the edge of the waves.

My father tells about going down to Santa Cruz with his family as a boy or to Carmel, where Uncle John (who was actually Grammy's uncle)—John who had come to America first, who had worked his way across the continent building the Canadian railroad—had a stone house that he'd built with his own hands. My skinny little sun-soaked father sat on the beach shivering from the cold water, bitten by sand fleas. And before my father there was the family homestead in the lit- tle village on the Norwegian fjord. I don't know why I like to think about my family so much—these people who came before me, whom I am so biologically close to but whose stories I will never know. I have pictures of all these Norwegian ancestors going back hundreds of years, lining the wall above my TV. One couple look like pilgrims, and one guy has a thick black beard and a balding head and one blue eye and one brown, and I think he must have been a lighthouse keeper, and I'm sure he knew the comfort of the waves.

⚜

I put *Emma* aside and started reading *Persuasion* again last night. I couldn't be in Lyme, on my way to Bath, and not read it. *Persuasion* just makes me happy—in a different way than *P&P.* It is quieter, not so "sparkling."[4] It's the product of an older Austen. How can anyone not love Anne? I am afraid, though, that I am too much like Mary, always thinking that someone else has something better—and always thinking myself ill and then eating more anyway.

Jane was so particular about men. This is what she says about Mr. Elliot, Anne's cousin who is trying to win her over:

> Mr. Elliot was rational, discreet, polished, but he was not open.
> There was never any burst of feeling, any warmth of indignation
> or delight, at the evil or good of others. This, to Anne, was a
> decided imperfection. Her early impressions were incurable. She
> prized the frank, the open-hearted, the eager character beyond
> all others. Warmth and enthusiasm did captivate her still. She
> felt that she could so much more depend upon the sincerity of
> those who sometimes looked or said a careless or a hasty thing,
> than of those whose presence of mind never varied, whose
> tongue never slipped.[5]

Jane attributes the feelings to Anne, but they must have been hers as well.

I am of two minds. One: if such a small failure as this is enough to disqualify a guy, how would anyone ever be good enough? And two: I am afraid about Jack, afraid this is his weakness, and afraid as a result that I cannot trust him.

He was always polished; he always said the right thing. (I know, I know. Now are we to fault guys for saying the right thing *and* for saying the wrong thing?) But it was almost like he knew precisely what would sound best in each situation, and that's what he said. A little too perfect.

There was one night, Monday, after we had sat by the river talking for so long, we walked back and went with a group to dinner at a little French crepe place. Greg, upon realizing that one of the guys who is a proctologist (or a "plumber," as he calls himself) was a captive audience, launched into a long and detailed story involving kidney stones, shunts, catheters, an intern, and no anesthetic. I needed sleep. The noise of the conversation was too much for me. The shunts were too much for me. I alternately cringed quietly and put forth a great deal of effort to be pleasant, to what I'm sure was little effect.

When we all first sat down, Sara said to Jack, "Do you want to sit across from your wife?" and I laughed and said, "Oh, we just met yesterday." Then he got this determined smile on his face and said in his kindest voice, "But thank you though." As if he couldn't imagine a better compliment. There was something about it. I sensed that he was probably cringing inside, but he would never let on. And I thought I would have to watch him, to see if he always said what he thought other people wanted to hear regardless of what he actually thought.

I don't know. Maybe I am tired and crazy. And maybe to make an issue of this would be overly particular. Anne was right about Mr. Elliot. He was only there for the money; he could not be trusted. Jack, I am almost sure, can be.

Sixteen

Sensibility and Self-Expression

*An interval of meditation, serious and grateful,
was the best corrective of everything dangerous
in such high-wrought felicity; and she went
to her room, and grew steadfast and fearless in the
thankfulness of her enjoyment.*

—PERSUASION

I found the perfect connection through Exeter, thrilled because Jane set *Sense and Sensibility* here—Barton Park was four miles north of Exeter, she says. So I looked out on Marianne's countryside; only I'd seen so many rolling hills and fields that I couldn't tell any of them apart anymore, and all of this looked just like the rest of England to me. Perhaps the hills were more gently rolling, or maybe they were higher and the fields darker green under a gray sky. My powers of observation were completely diminished, and I was convinced the other side of the train had all the gorgeous views. (Again feeling like Mary, "My seat is damp. I'm sure Louisa has found a better.")[1] And I became afraid all my clothes smelled of the frying oil of Lyme.

I thought of how I love gossipy, kindhearted Mrs. Jennings, grave Colonel Brandon, wholehearted Marianne, and Elinor, who always exerts herself to do what's right, to be civil to everyone, to think the best of people, never to give rein to her emotions—at least until she finds that Edward Ferrars had not married Lucy Steele and was free to propose to her. Then she herself "burst[s] into tears of joy."[2] "Her feelings were strong; but she knew how to govern them," Jane says.[3] Only Elinor's method of governing is at times one of exacting and empty precision, in deep sorrow to prevent herself from saying anything at all simply because she has made a promise to the ingratiating, fawning Lucy Steele.

In my own life I've had trouble negotiating the balance between selfishness and self-expression, which is the core conflict of the Dashwoods. It is, I think, one of the constant daily struggles in relationships—what to do with your emotions, how much to express them or subject others to them. I feel things more strongly than the rest of my family. My parents and my brother are matter-of-fact and even, and then there is me, with this extra bundle of pure emotion. If I look like both my parents, I don't feel the way they do. Emotionally, I think they may secretly wonder about my parentage. I have always wanted to be one of those easy happy people, and I think for a while I pretended to be that way, but really I am much more of an Eeyore. I think in some ways I will always be a mystery to them.

This is the one thing my mother and I fought about growing up. She felt that I was imposing my bad moods on others; I thought I should be allowed to be depressed or sad if that's what I was feeling. She wanted me to exert myself. I was probably being a moody teenager, taking my moods out on others, or maybe I was feeding my feelings à la

Marianne. But those arguments, combined with a Christian culture that is incredibly uncomfortable with lamentation and rushes to happiness, left me with an impression that only positive emotions are good and that everything else needed to be at a minimum subdued and sometimes covered over with smiles and cheerful voices, insincere thanksgiving and praise. There is a way to be sad or angry without overly imposing those emotions on others like a petulant teenager, of course, but I did not understand that at the time.

I don't mean to imply that evangelical Christians are emotionally disabled, but there is a strain of evangelicalism, particularly among women I think, in which anything that isn't happy is viewed as dangerous. I can't abide that anymore. It doesn't work for me. I cannot be part of a religion that doesn't understand lament.

I am still learning to just experience my feelings, to allow my emotions to simply be what they are without being afraid of them or trying to force them quickly into something else, still negotiating this balance in the course of everyday relationships. It is not an easy thing, at least not for me.

I catch hints of Elinor in Jane's letters. Family tradition is that Jane fainted when she came back home to Steventon from visiting Martha Lloyd and was told that her parents had decided to move the family to Bath.[4] She was twenty-five. It was the end of an era, the loss of her beloved family home (though it stayed in the family and went to her brother James, who took over as rector of Steventon from his father), her dear Hampshire countryside, and her small, steady group of friends. Moving furniture was not easy then, so they took very little with them, and Mr. Austen sold his library of five hundred books. In a sense, the Austens were repeating family history. Mrs. Austen's parents had moved to Bath when they retired; her father had died here.[5] She met George and married him shortly after her father's death—the hope of many parents who took their older daughters to Bath (not that they themselves would die, of course, but that their daughters would find husbands).

But Jane wrote to Cassandra with characteristic cheerfulness in January, to talk about where they might live in Bath and what they would take with them when they moved, saying she was "more & more reconciled to the idea of our removal," and maybe she was. Her letter is, as always, full of laughter. "We have lived long enough in this Neighbourhood, the Basingstoke Balls are certainly on the decline,"[6] she says. I wonder how deeply she felt this, how much she was exerting herself for the sake of her family. James Edward said that "depression was little in accordance with her nature,"[7] so maybe she never fell into any lengthy emotional depths.

Tradition, though, is that if she ever was depressed, it was here, a suspicion bolstered by the fact that she seems to have written very little during the Bath years. She recopied *Susan,* which later became *Northanger Abbey,* and started to work on *The Watsons*[8] but never finished it. She seems to have preferred not to be too much part of society, and living in Bath may have forced her out of her quiet daily routine. There were "tiny, stupid" parties that she hated because they required the exertion of talking to everyone and because the people were generally dull.[9] When she finally left five years later, it was "with what happy feelings of Escape!"[10]

In spite of dear Jane's experiences, I have come to be happy at Bath. It is raining. Ah, rain in Bath! How lovely. It always rains in Bath. The honey-colored Bath Stone buildings seem to glow. My room is gorgeous, decorated in pale greens and deep reds and mauves, with thick wallpaper and expensive bedding, which lacks the ring of dirt that was the particular distinction of the room in Lyme. The small *en suite* bath has lovely white tile, with only a bit of the kind of mold with which I am most familiar, the faint orange stuff that I cannot keep from growing on my shower at home.

My B&B—the Villa Magdala—is across Pulteney Bridge and just up the street from the stylish Laura Place,[11] the square of town houses where Lady Dalrymple stays in *Persuasion*. (Readers don't get to see much of Lady Dalrymple, but apparently the best thing about her to most concerned—particularly to her vain Elliot cousins—is that she is, in fact, a viscountess.)

I walk over half the city, around the abbey and by the baths, up toward the Circus and Royal Crescent, feeling the luxury of being here and being halfway through *Persuasion*. In the evening, beyond exhausted, I am lured out by the chance to see the green pools of the Roman Baths by torchlight.

⚜

I am wearing my jeans again. I have worn them every day since Margaret's, and now they are filthy. Every outfit I packed, I was thinking of Bath—which exists for shopping and being fashionable—and now it is too cold to wear them. Last night I wore my whole ensemble—jeans (of course) with a T-shirt, fleece, and Gore-Tex jacket, and I was still cold. I have no idea what the temperature is because of the Celsius-Fahrenheit conversion, which I can't be bothered to figure out.

Jane did not particularly enjoy fashion, according to tradition. Her letters are full of references to this or that muslin gown, or a new dress for a ball, or what she should buy for Cassandra in Bath for her new hat because fruit was now fashionable. So cherries or a plum?[12] Neither sounds like a particularly good idea. While she seems to have taken some pains, rumor is that she was not actually very good with clothes, and I think her main goal was simply to be acceptable. She doesn't seem to have hoped for—or unfortunately attained—anything more than that.

I think it took me thirty years to develop some sense of fashion, and I am officially mourning every outfit that will sit in my suitcase for the next four days while it rains in Bath. I used to think I had few regrets in my life, but now I realize that I have worn some very bad outfits, and particularly bad bathing suits, and I'm not sure what it says about my character that I regret this almost more than anything else.

I meandered aimlessly through Bath in my jeans and fleece, fighting off a bit of traveler's malaise. I sat in the abbey for the beginning of morning service, then headed back to the baths. There are multiple pools, the main bath with an open roof. Inside rooms include separate pools for men and women, an ancient hot tub, a massage room with heated floors. And all of this around the time of Christ. The Romans came here to worship the healing goddess Sulis Minerva, and there are remnants of the temple. They threw curses in the water, or prayers, but mostly curses it seems, for anyone who had offended them or who may have stolen their favorite amber pendant. Ridiculous but in some way satisfying I'm sure.

I walked up to the Royal Crescent, still the most fashionable address in Bath, a magnificent semicircle of grand Bath Stone town houses from the early eighteenth century, close to the top of the hill on which the city is built. Number 1, Royal Crescent is now a museum fitted up the way it would have been when the Duke of York,

George III's second son, lived here in 1776.[13] It is gorgeous, of course, but the thing that most struck me was a tiny little marble scratcher, like a back scratcher on a much smaller scale, that was used to help dig the bugs out from under one's wig. Apparently they rarely removed them and rarely washed their hair, and little things flourished under there. Wigs were going out of style in Jane's day, and men were laying off from powdering their hair, as well, and beginning to wear it short. When Jane's younger brother Charles opted to go cropped without any powder, it was an item of concern to his rather more posh brother Edward.

There are Austen remembrances around every corner. The center square contains the abbey and baths and Pump Room, which is now a restaurant and still has the fountain drawing up water from the baths for drinking—I don't think I will drink the water, though you still can—and a few little cafés. And then there are small alleys and wide streets with boutiques and restaurants and town houses. (I don't think there are any actual houses here in Bath, only town houses.) Most of the spots I know from Austen—Laura Place, the Circus, the Royal Crescent, Queen Square, where Edward stayed when he came to town—are all just various shapes of town house assortments. The Circus is a circle, of course, around a central green. (Doesn't the name make it sound like it should be more than just a place to live? Or like they all must live raucous lives there? It's terribly sedate for being called the Circus.) It seems like it would be a lovely thing to live in Bath.

Late in the afternoon I walked through Sydney Gardens and right by 4 Sydney Place, where the Austens first lived on coming here.[14] Sydney Place seems luxurious, as does most of Bath to me, but I was too tired to do more than venture into the edge of the park. Alas, there are none of the public breakfasts in Sydney Gardens that there were when Jane lived here, at least not this week. I expected there to be more entertainment in Bath—fireworks or concerts in the gardens. I've not found any outdoor entertainment (perhaps because of the rain) and nothing in the Assembly Rooms either. And nothing is free.

I sat on a bench eating fast food, watching a family play Frisbee, feeling very alone.

Saturday night I plan to go to the theater. They say I should be able to get a half-price ticket for ten pounds beforehand. They also say it's okay to wear jeans.

⌘

Sadly, I am unable to take a bath in Bath as my en suite has only a lovely tiny shower. One may visit the Baths, one may purchase all sorts of soaps and salts and gels, but one may not actually bathe.

Am completely and utterly distracted with thoughts of Jack. Afraid I've begun to think of him entirely as my own. Can barely read *Persuasion*. I'm too distracted with my own story—at times edging on panic, but mostly blissfully happy, ready to laugh for no real reason—like Anne, with "exquisite, though agitated sensations…, disposed…to be courteous and kind to all, and to pity every one, as being less happy than" myself.[15]

At times I have been more in dread and fear than anything else—that something should happen so quickly and surely, that my life could change so suddenly. Here I am jumping to conclusions again. I am afraid of either possibility, if it works out as it seems destined to or if it falls apart. I am entirely comfortable when I'm with him; why I should be uncomfortable apart from him I don't understand. He's given me no reason to be comfortable though.

I think we are incredibly, unbelievably blessed. To be in love with someone you believe in, whom you respect and who respects you back, with whom you share all basic values, who welcomes your intelligence, who shares your laughter. To have it be a sure thing, not something that is strong enough to convince you to hold on to it and weak enough to keep you from commitment, not caught in that horrible middle ground. If my experience bears out what my heart perceives, I expect to be able to love him quickly and without reserve.

Perhaps I am foolish to think that experience will fall in line with what I have imagined over the last two weeks. I had one week to get to know him and conclude that he was my ideal; he will have months to disappoint. (It may not take months to disappoint; a week will be sufficient if I don't hear from him.) I'm certain if he knew how much I think of him now he would be horrified. He's been in Jordan. I've been traipsing around England following Jane Austen and reading her novels. Argh! Try falling in love and then taking weeks to delve into Austen with the prescription that you really ought not to think about the guy you're in love with.

I really need to be more like Elinor, but Elinor had a reason to put all her hopes aside. She had Lucy; she knew for certain Edward was unavailable. I'm sure with that kind of certainty I could be brokenhearted and steely and move on. But I have no devastating certainty— only a girl in North Carolina he may or may not be dating.

I don't have to know any of this now, any of the things my heart seems to be certain about. I can just relax and enjoy right where we are, which is just a beginning, and see where things go. I expect things to go swimmingly. I expect to laugh. I expect to have great conversations. I expect him to be kind and gentle. I expect my family to love him and my mother to be giddy and everyone else to wholeheartedly approve.

I will be home in ten days, and my time here is too valuable to be consumed thinking only about him. One way or the other, when I get home something will happen—or not happen—and I will have my answer.

I think about Jane meeting someone at the coast, finding him a match, Cassandra expecting him to be successful, Jane waiting to hear from him and only getting notice of his death. Jack flew home today, and I prayed for his safety. I can't imagine if that were the end of it all. I can't imagine what Jane felt.

I have been tired all day, and now that it is ten minutes after eleven, I don't know that I will be able to sleep. This waiting is a tender kind of torture. This bed is too big and gorgeous to be achingly empty.

Seventeen

The Bath Bun

Remember that we are English,
that we are Christians.

—HENRY TILNEY, *NORTHANGER ABBEY*

From the top of Beechen Cliff, the whole city of Bath is a beautiful crowd of Bath Stone buildings in a neat jumble below, from Camden Place at the top, to the abbey in the middle and all the way down to the river. I hiked the nearly deserted path, covered over by trees, past town houses whose backyard gardens have the most amazing views. The climb was torturous but worth it. Sweet Catherine Morland hikes Beechen Cliff with Henry and Eleanor Tilney in *Northanger Abbey* while Henry lectures her on the picturesque, so that when she gets to the top, no longer trusting her own ideas of beauty, she "voluntarily reject[s] the whole city of Bath, as unworthy to make part of a landscape."[1]

Northanger Abbey is so much fun, but I think fewer people read it, which is a shame. It's a satire of the gothic romances of the time, all the skeletons and villains and crazy women wrongfully locked away for years on end. Catherine's trip to Bath is her first entrée into the world, and she is too good-hearted herself to fully understand anyone's real character, full of seventeen-year-old naive enthusiasm and imagination, so she gets into a few scrapes. When she goes home with her new friends the Tilneys—who are gracious and kind, except for their father—she is enthralled with their home, the old abbey (though it is not nearly dark or dirty enough for her gothic tastes), and imagines herself into all kinds of ridiculous situations. The worst is when she goes to look for their dead mother, whom she thinks may be still alive and kept shut away by the colonel in a bedroom in the old part of the house or perhaps was horribly murdered by him when the children were all away. She is found out there by Henry, and as it turns out, the colonel is actually mean-hearted, not enough to kill his wife, but enough to cruelly send Catherine away alone when he realizes she's not so rich as he was led to believe.

Of course, Catherine eventually marries Henry Tilney. I think this is Jane's most realistic match. Henry doesn't have any violent romantic emotions, though he is "sincerely attached to her" and "truly love[s] her society." Jane says "his affection originated in nothing better than gratitude, or, in other words, that a persuasion of her partiality for him had been the only cause of giving her a serious thought."[2] Not a grand love, but a steady one.

I hike back down to the center of town and the Bath Bun Tea Room for cream tea and *Persuasion*. It finishes so beautifully here. Anne gets a glow back in her complexion and her spirit. The Musgroves come to stay at the White Hart (which was a real inn, across a little promenade from the Baths), and Mary is actually thrilled to be in Bath, verging on happiness. Mrs. Russell is there, but Anne is now stronger, able to counter her sometimes mistaken advice. The Admiral and Mrs. Croft are delighted to be in Bath and to see Anne, and you begin to feel that she actually does have friends in the world. And then Captain Wentworth realizes that he's been proud and a little ridiculous, that he has wasted years by not coming back to Anne sooner, by not asking her to marry him again after he had established himself with more of an income. His pride was hurt, so he determined never to come back. Only he finds that impossible once he has a hint of Anne's feelings from that wonderful conversation with Captain Harville while Captain Wentworth sat nearby writing a letter. "We certainly do not forget you so soon as you forget us," Anne says. "It is, perhaps, our fate rather than our merit. We cannot help ourselves."[3] And then Wentworth cannot stand it any longer and pours out his heart, and everything is sealed on a quiet walk on the gravel path behind the Circus. I would like to find that gravel path.

I'm afraid my own failures, like Anne's, have been more of personality rather than morality. Not that that's something to entirely brag about. Perhaps I have not been brave enough to sin, and maybe that is not entirely a moral victory.[4]

I've been consumed with my own failures—fashion and otherwise—over the last few years. I don't know why. Sometimes when I can't sleep, they run over and over through my mind, and there are enough of them to go on and on in that state. Sometimes I just fester on one of them for an hour, so consumed with its immensity that thoughts of any others are just reminders that there are other cavernous pits in my memory. My father says I worry about everything, but he doesn't really know the half of it.

I was born compliant, wanting to make other people happy, like Catherine unsure that my own views of the world were worth expressing. I wasn't always strong enough to go after what I wanted. I made decisions to please my parents, or because it was what was generally expected of me, or because it was easy. I was too insecure to hear any kind of criticism without it making me hurt and angry, but on the other hand I think there has always been a constant critic in my head. I have generally not been brave. I am now, I think, but I wasn't always. I feel like it took me longer than average to grow up. I think I'm not alone in feeling that way. There were parts of my life that were not fully lived because I was timid and afraid. (And, of course, a bit of a nerd. I will always be a bit of a nerd in the best possible sense.)

But today is not a day for feeling failure. Today I'm brave and full of peace. If anything, at the moment I'm startled by loving life. I'm daring now (at least a little), and I get to live my dream, to be a writer. (People ask me, "What do you do?" And I say, "I'm a writer," and still it surprises me.) My life is full of possibility, and when I get home, however things work out with Jack doesn't really seem to matter. Not today.

So, like Catherine, I have nothing to do but "forgive [myself] and be happier than ever."[5]

⁂

I've made a mess with my tea and I am wet, but I couldn't care less. I'm back at the Bath Bun, this time with cream tea and *Emma,* sitting outside under a big blue umbrella. It's so quiet and nice here in the soft rain. This is my favorite spot in Bath.

I worked up the strength to walk uptown to St. Swithin's, the small church where Mr. and Mrs. Austen were married and where Mr. Austen is buried, as well as Jane's grandfather, her mother's father. It was locked, so I couldn't get in, but peering through the iron gate in

the cold rain, I could see Mr. Austen's memorial stone in the churchyard. Fanny Burney's memorial is there too, author of *Camilla* and
Cecilia and *Evelina,* books Jane loved.

If Jane didn't love Bath already, her father's death gave her less reason still to like it. He died on January 21, 1805, at the age of seventy-
three.[6] (Her dear friend Anne Lefroy had died just a month earlier in a
riding accident.[7]) Jane wrote to her brother Frank on the HMS *Leop-
ard* to let him know about their father's death and unfortunately had to
write to break the news to him two separate times because she had
some misinformation about the ship's location. George Austen fell ill
on Saturday, with "an oppression in the head with fever, violent tremu-
lousness, & the greatest degree of Feebleness." Sunday he seemed much
recovered, but that afternoon he took a turn for the worse, and by
Monday, Dr. Gibbs was declaring that "nothing but a Miracle could
save him."[8] That morning her father passed away.

Jane writes of "his virtuous & happy life," and says, "The loss of
such a Parent must be felt, or we should be Brutes—"[9] And then in her
next letter: "His tenderness as a Father, who can do justice to?"[10]

George Austen was faithful and full of good humor and an excellent father. He loved his family, cared for his children, worked hard at
being rector of a country parish. He seems to have had a genuine faith
and no doubt worked to instill this in all of his children. We know that
Jane copied out sermons for him from time to time.[11] I think she was
not the type to simply write things out without commenting on them,
particularly if she disagreed, so you can imagine that they may have discussed theological issues as well. And while it wasn't the style then to
educate daughters much, the girls had access to their father's extensive
library, and the family was always reading to one another in the evening.

The man who spent years teaching ancient Greek and Latin was not above loving lowbrow novels. He was the kind of father who worked to get his sons' advancement in the navy and reminded Frank when he left home at fourteen of the importance not only of prayer but of cleaning one's teeth in a letter Frank cherished all his life, which was found "water-stained…and frayed by constant reading" after Frank's death at ninety-one.[12] And her father was the first to attempt to publish one of Jane's books, convinced that *First Impressions* was good enough for a wider audience than just the family.

No doubt Jane got many of her ideas about being a country clergyman from her father. It was a time in which church positions were traded almost like stock in a business. They often went to the highest bidder, who would hire someone for as little as possible to actually show up and do the church services. Mr. Austen believed contrarily that a country rector was really no good unless he lived among his people, that there was much good to be done just living out love on a day-to-day basis, setting an example of faithfulness. Edmund gives voice to all of these opinions in *Mansfield Park,* concluding that "as the clergy are, or are not what they ought to be, so are the rest of the nation."[13]

The faith of the Austens was in many ways unusual, for it was an age in which being English meant being Christian, and being Christian often meant no more than being English. At the other extreme, there was the new Methodist movement, sincere in their faith and sometimes very severe. Had Jane been at either end of this spectrum, her writing would not be what it is. Had she been in a Methodist family, she may have been too serious to enjoy the frivolity of plays and novels. She ended up being very faithful, with a great deal of common sense (not to impugn the Methodists, of course) and an appreciation for humor and joy. I think in many ways she owed that to her father.

Necessarily, as children and parents, our perspectives on each other are slightly skewed. In some ways we see each other better than anyone else because we have the closeness of everyday life in which to observe every fault and every goodness, but the faults are more apparent somehow. In some ways, we get into patterns of thinking about each other, and it's hard to get out of those ruts and see each other as we really are. There is always an undercurrent, which we try to read and interpret and sometimes ignore—all these exhausting perceptions.

I've always been thankful for my particular parents, though I feel like now that they are in their early sixties I'm only beginning to understand their worth.

My father is a country rector of sorts. After retiring from the air force, he went to work full time for our church, an independent Bible church in the D.C. suburbs. And he has just retired from that to actually retire. He is wise and incredibly kind, and the years have brought out a great gentleness in him, or maybe it was there and I never saw it before.

My mom and I have always connected—for good or bad, but mostly for good—on an emotional level, easily and naturally. My father and I are so different that it took me longer to understand his perfections. Getting to have a closer relationship with him now is one of the joys of my life.

There is one aspect to *Emma* that always bothers me. It is the two days she spends in agony wondering about how Knightley feels after she realizes that she has always loved him and can't stand the thought of his marrying Harriet, if indeed he could be contemplating that. It's not what Emma feels, or how those feelings are described; it's that she has to wait only two days to find out that Knightley loves her equally in return. Once again, Emma gets exactly what she wants, with little difficulty (which I think is just the thing Jane thought no one would like about her). It's not that I don't like Emma. But I don't feel much pity for her seeing how everything was so quickly resolved.

Relationships in Jane's day happened so much faster. Mr. Collins proposed to Lizzy in little more than a week (and then, of course, to Charlotte Lucas just a few days later). Knightley and Emma went from being friends to being engaged in the space of five minutes. Marianne and Willoughby were the closest to dating, hanging out together inseparably, but even he was ready to propose within two months at the most. This is an extreme I wouldn't want to go back to, nor would I want the kind of world in which Charlotte Lucas's accepting Mr. Collins makes any kind of sense whatsoever. But today we've gone to another extreme. We date for years, only to have (usually) the guy unable to make up his mind, unable to finally commit. I can kind of understand this when couples are living together and there's no real need for commitment, but within the church, without being too hard on the guys (because who wants to encourage someone into marriage who isn't ready for it?), I suppose I expect them to be more masculine, to prize marriage more, to be better able to commit.

So we have all these Christian couples going out for years and attempting not to have sex. Personally, I'm about ready to try one of the other extremes—to marry someone ridiculously fast or to just give up and move in with someone. I have no intention of doing that, of course, but I can't say it's not attractive.

❦

I am exhausted (I'm always exhausted) and beginning to feel ready to go home. I don't want to leave Bath. My eyes are bloodshot. There are bags underneath them that I cannot cover up. I am dying to talk to someone close to me, and if anyone at the hotel or at church is too nice, I am likely to burst into tears. I don't have the energy to exert myself anymore, all of this traveling alone. My ankles hurt.

Why did I bring twelve pounds of books? They don't fit in my bags.

Just when I was in need of care, the sermon at St. Michael's was on 1 Peter 5:6–7: "Humble yourselves therefore under the mighty hand of God, so that he may exalt you in due time. Cast all your anxiety on him, because he cares for you."

I'm still trying to get my head around what it means to trust God. For some reason I fear that God would just as soon (or even rather) rake me over the coals than give me something that feels genuinely good, something I really want. As though now that I've seen that side of God, I can't allow him to be good in the way we define goodness. I'm not sure why I feel this so strongly; it's not like I am Job, with a list of grievances. I keep thinking about Jane's prayer: "We feel that we have been blessed far beyond any thing that we have deserved; and though we cannot but pray for a continuance of all these mercies, we acknowledge our unworthiness of them and implore thee to pardon the presumption of our desires."[14] Seen from the right angle, there's a desperation in that, a feeling that perhaps you are dealing with a God who may be capricious at times, whose favor may not last. He cares for you. I'm trying to believe that.

And somehow now I feel him caring for me. There have been so many instances of grace and goodness on this trip. I want to pray, *I don't deserve this, but please give me more.*

I was dying for someone to welcome me at church, but that is not really the English way. But they sang one of my favorite songs at the end, and when I left to do some shopping, I was smiling scandalously at people on the street.

The theater was nice last night—smaller than any back home, but elegant and red. It was *Much Ado About Nothing.* I sat in the dress circle—of course, no one was wearing dresses—with an empty seat beside me and could barely get comfortable because my legs ached. It was a bit cruel to have to listen to Benedick, with his, "When I said I would die a bachelor, I did not think I should live till I were married."[15]

Against my will it made me think of Jack and wonder if he has quite determined not to marry. It is as though Elinor and Marianne are at war inside me—the one determined not to think about him (I have no real reason to after all) and the other all smiles and hopes. I am leaving all thoughts of him in Bath and determined they will not follow me. Derbyshire sounds terribly romantic I think. If only I felt like going anywhere. I'm staying at a pub and it will probably smell.

Eighteen

Pilsley and Pemberley
(Or What Makes Darcy Great)

But there certainly are not so many men
of large fortune in the world,
as there are pretty women to deserve them.

—MANSFIELD PARK

The village of Pilsley is tiny and I adore it. I sat on my sloping canopy bed looking out the window on two or three streets, all the cottages of stone, every one with a garden, and all the doors and trim painted the loveliest shade of teal blue—even the little schoolhouse at the end of the street. It's very clean and everything a pub should be—red carpet and thick beams, comfortable clutter everywhere. So as a result, all is better than right with the world. There are even two sweet brown English Labs.

I called home and talked to my parents and each of my nieces—the twins are three, and Grace is getting close to five—and they want to know when I am going to come see them, which makes me miss them even more. They manage at the same time to be both terrors and the sweetest children in the world. They are very loud, which I love, and regularly get into very bad trouble. As my sister says, it's a good thing they're cute.

Being an aunt has been one of the best surprises of my life. I cannot make up fairy stories like Jane did for her nieces and nephews, but I read stories to them and buy them things and let them eat whatever they want, and this seems to make up for any other deficiencies in their minds. Grace is terribly put upon having two younger sisters. She said her first sentence when she was about sixteen months and Linda was in the hospital with the twins: "Dog poop 'side," like she was finally beginning to understand the world, and this was so interesting to her, seeing the dog pooping in the backyard.

Alison has a little smoker's voice. We don't know where she got it. I want to always remember her singing her grace before dinner ("God our Father, God our Father, we thank you…") sounding like she'd just finished a pack of Marlboros. Once I took Eleanor to Frying Pan Park, a little farm by my house, and before we even pulled up she started to laugh in her car seat—she was two and a half I think—like I've never heard a little child laugh, continuous, genuine joy. Once she got over the great wonder of finding thousands of small rocks in the parking lot (she was collecting them then), she continued her laughing spree all around the barnyard, interspersed with animal noises ("Heheheheh, pig! pig! oink, oink, oink, hehehehheh, cow! moooooo").

Ellie and Ali, the twins, are sort of miracle babies. They are identical and there was only one sac, which is rare and dangerous. Linda was in the hospital for ten weeks before they were born. Had the timing for the separation of the egg been only slightly different, they would have been conjoined. So they were born early, tiny and with acid reflux so bad that Jon and Linda had to shove feeding tubes down their noses and pump them with formula. They screamed for the first five months of their lives, louder than any babies I've ever heard. It's still their first reaction to anything unpleasant—real or imagined.

Anyway, it's all great fun for me because I just get to hear the stories and give them things and love them. And they adore me, which is pretty much the best deal in the world.

I've always wanted to have children. I hope I will. Every year I cower at the doctor's office (not any doctor but *that* doctor, you know), wrapped in something that looks like a big paper towel with armholes and a huge rip down the front, trying to keep my intricate parts covered. The walls are pinned with pictures of delivery-room moms, smiling and sweaty, holding prizeling prune-faced babies, surrounded by three or four or five stairstep kids. The women glow, as if they've just fulfilled their earthly mission. They've gotten these bits and pieces of intricate wiring and odd-shaped containers to actually produce something valuable— something human. How could you ever ask anything of them again? They've done their life's best work. I would like one or two or three little prizeling babies of my own. And if not, I think perhaps I'll adopt one, a girl, maybe with brown skin and curly hair, or maybe very shy.

I was worried about how I would get here, to the pub. I took the train to Matlock, which is about fifteen minutes away, and walked to the bus station, but the schedules were very hard to read, and it was nearly deserted except for one rather shady character. A cab just happened to pull up with the sweetest driver. He was thin, Pakistani, and barely spoke English, probably late thirties. He couldn't pronounce the name Pilsley or even spell it, but he was so enthusiastic to take me here and managed to follow the signs without any problem and pointed out the great Chatsworth estate along the way. It seems that his parents live here in England, too, and that he and his wife have no children, which is a shame because I'm sure he would shower them with great and demonstrative affection.

⚜

My wonderful dumpy bed is once again achingly empty. My bed is always empty. It is one of the things about my life that seems ridiculous in the twenty-first century that would not have seemed so to Jane.

It's not that I don't want to have sex; it's not even that all the desires are repressed and buttoned up. They are just there, and I bide them. I wait with them. I endure them. At the risk of sounding cheesy or ridiculously holy, I give them to God. Sometimes I do not want to give them to God. Sometimes I just weep them at him or with him, try to make sure he is hearing me struggle at least. Biblically, of course, he is with me in the struggle, but his presence is not as palpable as I'd like. He can be a thin sort of thing when I need a physical presence. Half the time it seems crazy, even to me, and I'm afraid that if the right guy came along—someone charming and funny, who adored me—I could just forget it all. I'm afraid of that.

Tonight I want Jack to be here. I'm not supposed to be thinking about him, but I can't stop.

I don't regret pursuing chastity. I'm not sorry that this is how I've lived my life. But in the present and future, it's harder to be certain. I believe this is the right decision and the healthiest decision, the intention of God's creation and the best way to fulfill it (if one can talk about being fulfilled not having sex) and all that. It's just that it doesn't always make sense.

More than anything else, this one aspect of my life throws into stark relief the fact that I am not living for myself. It is the central tenet of Christianity—your life is not your own; it is not solely about your pleasure but about serving and obeying God. I've never thought that anyone outside the church had any reason to attempt this lifestyle—I mean, there are other reasons, but making people who don't profess Christianity feel guilty about their life choices is not my thing. Not that they aren't good general principles, but the moral strictures of the faith are for those within the faith, not those outside. Sometimes I think, like the apostle Paul said, if we are wrong in the end, we will have been crazy indeed. This is when I doubt my faith the most. Sometimes the desire to be normal—and not be alone—overcomes almost everything else.

My innocent Christian college friend Kari has given up. She was visiting for a couple of weeks and met a guy and just didn't come home. I wouldn't even have known if she hadn't told me. She said he had a talent for caustic sarcasm and didn't like his family much and had a master's degree in Italian literature and that she adored him. For a while she slunk away, dodging shame when she saw me, and then whatever shame was there seemed replaced by loud happiness. She's attempted to hold on to both her strict faith and her adoring boyfriend, and I have to believe she's uncomfortable with the tension. I have to believe there is tension.

I could so easily do the same thing. Actually, I think sometimes that had the opportunity been reversed, she would have been the one counseling me about the soul-bruising effects of sin. But mostly I'm afraid for her, afraid that this particular means of happiness will fail her, maybe spectacularly.

The prospect of possibly not being alone forever—this impossible lonely marathon being nearly over—has me giddy tonight in this slouchy bed.

❧

I just paid ten pence (*P*, as they're called) for a vile toilet at the Disley train station, but it was worth every *P*. My goal is Lyme Park—Colin Firth's Pemberley—but I have one mile to walk, and since today has been a comedy of errors already, I am beginning to fear that it will be as illusory as Godmersham. I have visions of disappearing sidewalks and having to flag a car down in the rain.

I adore that movie, the BBC version of *P&P*, perhaps in a manner that borders on being excessive and slightly irrational. I want to see the approach to the house, which is one of the best moments, when Elizabeth and the Gardiners come through the trees and see it for the first time across the lake.

It's taken me more than three hours to get here, most of the last hour trying to talk myself out of having to pee so badly. I only realized after getting on the bus for Disley that I had to go to the bathroom very bad. I wonder, does anything bad happen if you wait to pee longer than you should? I heard a story once in high school about a girl who waited so long to go that she couldn't go any more at all.

I hurried out of the pub this morning to catch a bus to Bakewell, to catch another bus to Buxton, to get a train to Disley. I had no idea it would be this hard. The bus should have come at 9:43, but it wasn't there by 9:45, then 9:47, then 9:52, and 10:12. Finally at 10:34 a bus arrived to find me first verging on panic and then incredibly relieved. The driver said the first one "musta broke down or something." On getting to Bakewell and after some difficulty finding the proper stand, I discovered another bus that would take me through Buxton and all the way here. It was a lovely ride, green hills, spectacular views, the occasional quarry—me wondering how many tiny villages the bus had to stop in and trying to convince myself that I could absolutely survive one hour. This is considered the Peak District, but I don't actually see any real peaks, though everything is bigger and grander here.

Lyme Park is actually right where it is supposed to be, with a wide sidewalk the entire way and a shuttle from the gate to the house. I had a picnic lunch and wandered through the gardens for a little over an hour. There's a long path around the lake, manicured flower gardens, an orangery. Close to the house is a sunken geometric Dutch garden with a detailed pattern of flowers and plants, but you can only look down on it and not actually walk through it. It's all lovely and understated, if not quite so grand as I imagined it to be—just kind of quietly gorgeous.

There used to be a little tour here showing significant spots in the movie, but when I asked about it in the information office, they said, "As it was filmed ten years ago, all of that has been taken down." You don't seem to be able to get to the spot where Darcy dives into the lake. It's back in a meadow beyond the official walking trails. The approach to the house is just as beautiful in real life. It's actually a view of the back of the house; it would be impossible to drive a carriage up that way.

At the risk of betraying the depth of my obsession with the film, I looked for the steps Darcy runs down on his way to meet the Gardiners and Elizabeth and the spot in the drive behind the house where their conversation was shot.

What exactly is it that makes Darcy so darn attractive? I think there's more going on here than just proud rich man falls in love with poor, spirited girl. For me so much of it is about his character—that he cares about it, for one thing, that he's concerned about being proud. That he not only takes Elizabeth's correction to heart but loves her for it.

I love the quote from Darcy's housekeeper, that he was "the best landlord and the best master...that ever lived. Not like the wild young men nowadays who think of nothing but themselves."[1] And Emma's dear Mr. Knightley knew what it meant to invest in the social welfare of those beneath him. One of my favorite quotes from Jane is from a letter to her niece, Fanny, who was just at the stage of deciding about suitors. Jane writes, "There are such beings in the World, perhaps, one in a Thousand, as the Creature You & I should think perfection, where Grace & Spirit are united to Worth, where the Manners are equal to the Heart & Understanding, but such a person may not come in your way."[2] That is just how I feel, and I'm afraid these men may be rarer today than they were then.

We don't value character much anymore. Being a gentleman is a lost art—and I suppose we don't really reward anyone for that. If they make us laugh or dress well or are good in bed, those are the things we've come to prize. But I think most women I know would take Darcy any day (of the Firth or Macfadyen variety), although they probably can't put into words what Darcy has that they're missing.

I find myself wondering about my deep connection to Austen's heroines as well—women who couldn't have professions, who were dependent on marriage or inheritance for their value in life, and who were basically forbidden from expressing their emotions to the men they loved. Yet hundreds of years beyond Austen, whether or not a woman marries and how successful that marriage is is still the defining characteristic of her life.

I used to think that there was a particular brand of Austenian marriage angst that was limited to the evangelical Christian community. Living in the evangelical culture, in which marriage and motherhood are still the prized roles for women, in which sex is put on hold until after the marriage vows, and in which men are still largely expected to take the lead in relationships, can give one a sense of kinship with Austen's early-nineteenth-century heroines, however different our situations in life.

Relationship discussions with my girlfriends center on trying to navigate a world in which we have little control, the rules are uncertain, and we are at times desperate. There are endless questions: *If I call him before he calls me, will he think I'm trying to take the lead and will that ruin everything? If we've been dating for years and he's unsure about marriage, is he a noncommittal loser or just waiting for God's direction? And if he seems to have led me on, is he weak-charactered or simply confused?*

I used to think these particular machinations were our own, that somehow the girls out there who were wearing Manolos and having sex and moving in with guys were too sophisticated to care about analyzing e-mails for signs of commitment-phobia. And then I watched *Sex and the City.* And there were Carrie and Miranda and Charlotte and Samantha—the girls who were going to try to have sex like guys, without feeling anything—analyzing conversations to try to figure out if Mr. Big's "I miss you, babe" was some sort of coded *mea culpa* and hoping (oh God, please) for something more substantial and long term than a brief, albeit incredibly good, one-night stand. Significantly, the producers chose to end the series with all of the characters in long-term relationships.

In many ways, we women live in our own world, a world where we analyze men and try to figure out how to get what we want from them and how to live with what we get from them. It makes me think of Eve's "your desire shall be for your husband"[3] curse. As Carrie would say,

"I am someone who is looking for love. Real love. Ridiculous, inconvenient, consuming, can't-live-without-each-other love." Only I am afraid that Mr. Big was no Mr. Darcy, and I wonder how much progress we've really made.

When I get home to the pub after another three hours on various buses, James, Rod and Jo's neighbor, tells me it would have taken only forty-five minutes in a car to get to Lyme Park. I think James comes here every night for a pint because this is his "local," as they say. I enjoy peering in on their world. Why ever don't we have pubs in America? Or cozy little villages? When I think of England, these are the things I think of. And tea shops. When I think of America, I think of oversized strip malls and chain restaurants. It's all very depressing.

❧

I'm lying on my back on the lawn behind Chatsworth watching the Emperor Fountain (close to where Matthew Macfadyen snogs Keira Knightley in the latest version of *P&P*). The sky is brilliant blue with only the occasional cloud, and after weeks of wrapping up I'm warm again, in my orange T-shirt and jean shorts. I'm probably getting sunburned, and it feels very good. A pair of squabbling ducks are creating a general commotion, and there's a couple just down from me who are so easy with each other, her head on his stomach, now and then sitting up and talking about what they should do for dinner, that for just a minute I wish I had company. But why be unhappy in a garden like this? Especially when there's ice cream.

I was enthralled with the house this morning when I first arrived. You can't see the whole thing at first because you walk up to it from the side, and from that direction it's hidden, so you discover its vastness gradually. But I quickly lost interest and decided I was in no mood to be entertained by an overdone 450-year-old homestead. I found myself turning up my nose at the elaborate paintings on every ceiling, the ornate furniture, the huge heavy silver chandelier celebrating the family's promotion to the dukehood, a room paneled with heavy oak carvings, stone tablets from ancient Egypt, a sculpture room full of delicate marble. The house is bigger and more magnificent than any I've seen, and at the beginning of the trip I could have given it its due, but at this point I've seen far too much to take in anything more. I found myself most interested by the views of the garden from the windows on the second floor.

There was one surprise that enchanted me—a set of china that had belonged to Warren Hastings, head of the East India Company. I generally don't go for those fancy kind of things, but this was lovely, with all kinds of different birds painted in the center of every plate and butterflies scattered around the edge and on the tip of every knife and fork, which are also done in china. Hastings's connection to the Austen family is a bit complicated, and there are debates about exactly the role he played. Jane's aunt Philadelphia, her father's sister, who was also (obviously) orphaned at a young age, found herself at twenty-one without marriage prospects in England and decided to leave for India, where lots of men were making their fortunes in the growing East India Company and where women were relatively scarce. Phila accomplished her objective, marrying Tysoe Saul Hancock, an older surgeon—actually the marriage may even have been arranged before she left England. Hancock seems to have been one of the unluckiest men ever. Nearly every business venture failed, friends deserted him, nothing ever really worked out, and he found virtually no success in what seems to have been a very hard and hard-working life. One of the couple's closest friends happened to be Warren Hastings—the very Warren Hastings who owned the lovely birds-and-butterflies china—who would rise through the ranks to eventually run the East India Company, be governor general of India, and make a fortune doing so.[4]

Phila and Hancock went without having children for years, and when Elizabeth eventually came along—well, there is speculation that perhaps she was actually Hastings's child. It seems a bad thing to speculate like this about the dead, who cannot defend themselves. The whole story may have just been, as Le Faye suggests, concocted by a gossipy old woman in Calcutta with a grudge. But I can't help but wonder, what really happened? Hastings was young, good-looking, and kind, a grieving widower. He sent his young son to live with the Austen family at Steventon in the early days when they had no children of their own, but the boy caught diphtheria and died, much to Mrs. Austen's grief. At any rate, Hastings was officially Elizabeth's godfather. He gave her enough of a living to keep her and her mother comfortable, though he married again and doesn't seem to have had a great deal of contact with the family. His taste in china was better than Edward's.

I can't do the garden justice. I've heard Chatsworth described as the Disneyland of manor houses, and there's an element of that (there are no free tours of the house, no free garden maps, and 2.75 pounds will buy you the tiniest roast beef sandwich ever). But a Disneyland of gardens—well, what's the harm in that? In addition to the Emperor Fountain, this huge jet of water over a long reflecting pool, there are kitchen gardens, a rose garden with Grecian columns, a sculpted maze, rocks and fountains and flowers throughout the hundred acres, all carefully placed. In the back are ponds with rambling (but no doubt managed) overgrowth, almost completely secluded from the rest. Everyone's favorite is the Cascade, a gentle, wide waterfall starting in a temple of sorts and flowing down toward the house over twenty-four sets of steps, all of different widths so that the sound of the water changes all the way down. Today it's full of parents and small children in their underwear (the children of course, not the parents). The garden rises behind the house, so there are spectacular views of the whole of Chatsworth and the rolling, sheep-strewn hills beyond.

There is some question about whether Jane was ever here at Chatsworth. Some believe she visited with cousins on a trip north, that perhaps it could have been a model for Pemberley (how many houses claim that?), but there is no proof she was ever here. Leading Austen scholar Deirdre Le Faye believes the farthest north Jane ever got was Staffordshire,[5] just west of Derbyshire, and that was after her father died, which would have been after she drafted *P&P* but before she edited it for publication. If she had seen it, it would have been quite different, but the Cascade would have been there, and the Seahorse Fountain, the long Cascade Pool, and the Grotto Pond. Capability Brown worked on the property in the 1700s at a cost of forty thousand pounds. Perhaps Austen was thinking of Brown when she wrote of the stream in front of Pemberley, "of some natural importance...swelled into greater, but without any artificial appearance."[6] That seems to have been one of his trademarks.

Lying here by the fountain makes me think of Elizabeth and Darcy. It makes me feel what she might have felt at seeing the evidence of the wealth she had only heard of before. When she and her aunt and uncle Gardiner apply to the housekeeper for a tour of Pemberley, Elizabeth finds herself looking out the windows at the river and valley, impressed by the rooms, which are done up with far more taste than Rosings Park, amazed by the vastness and elegant taste of it all. "Of this place I might have been mistress!" she thinks.[7] Austen weaves this discovery together with the revelations of Darcy's character—first Elizabeth learns that the housemaid adores Darcy and has never had an unkind word of him, that she has never seen anything of pride in him, and that he is the best brother imaginable. It seems that Elizabeth fell in love with Darcy's character and his estate on the same day. I wonder, which had greater influence?

Of course, we know that Elizabeth never could have loved him for the house and grounds and exalted position alone. Without some indication of better substance, Darcy would have been only a horrible man with a great house. But the discovery of the one must have made the other easier to swallow. And as they happen together, Austen leaves the motives a bit mixed, as they are in real life—do any of us know for certain why we really do anything we do?

We will never actually know what happened with Warren Hastings and Phila Austen Hancock. And we will never entirely ferret out our own motivations for anything we do. For my part, I want to believe that Hastings was innocent.

Nineteen

Over Hill and Dale

Nobody can tell what I suffer!

—MRS. BENNET, *PRIDE AND PREJUDICE*

Sitting outside a smelly pub in Youlgreave, eating in spitting rain, I watched the sun peek out from time to time, and it was a little too cold. I'd given up thinking about Jack, as it seemed I'd never get home and never see him again, stuck as I was in a youth hostel in England. I was feeling incredibly discouraged that my trip actually would come to an end. I wasn't ready to leave.

The view out my dorm room window is one of the most beautiful things I've ever seen, green hills under a wide sky, but one of my roommates snores, and the window rattles, and I cannot sleep.

Yesterday there were drama-queen tears, but I felt them even though I knew I was being slightly dramatic. I had carried my ridiculous suitcase up three of the steepest flights of stairs possible, thinking I should have stayed at the pub in Pilsley. I was incredibly disheartened to find that I can't do laundry here, can't check my e-mail, and the very helpful staff member who was determined to help me get to Ilam Hall—the whole point of coming here—now seems to think it "quite a trek," enough of a trek as to be seemingly impossible. I'd determined to take a day off and rest anyway, not wanting to tackle another three hours worth of buses through Bakewell and Ashbourne or whatever, but on being told it is nearly impossible to do this, I was heartbroken all over again—like breaking up with someone only to have them tell you they didn't want to go out anymore anyway. All my clothes are vile. I washed my socks and underwear in the sink and had a tiny pity party in my bunk, surrounded by wet things. I was on the edge of an emotional cliff when the clerk at the front desk reached out and pushed me right on over. I don't have the heart for this.

Ilam is supposed to be beautiful, quieter than Chatsworth or Lyme Park and with grounds that remarkably resemble Jane's Pemberley description, though I sort of doubt she was ever there.

I spent an hour walking through the dale this morning. You have to hike down a steep path to get to the main walking path, which runs by a little stream around hills and cliffs, with occasional breaks for panoramic views of cliff-side towns miles away. I was nearly alone, save for the horses and sheep. I am determined to think it is not a bad place to be stuck for the day.

So I sit here in the occasional rain, eating a ham and cheese toastie with chips and a salad with no dressing. The idea of a toastie does not bother me—sort of like grilled cheese without the butter—but I don't understand why no one here uses salad dressing. They sell it apparently, every kind you can imagine, only they forget to actually use it.

I'm tired of eating. I love food, but all the being hungry and constantly having to figure out where the next meal will come from—I mean, not financially, though there are enough questions about my finances to keep me occupied if I start to think about them, but practically. I've had some of the best meals here. Margaret's salmon with cream sauce with new potatoes and peas. At the abbey, roast beef and Yorkshire pudding, and the best lemon meringue pie I've ever had, with a creamy, custardy top—and I don't even like lemon meringue pie. Bath buns—light with chunky sugar on top, with lemon curd and clotted cream. And last night I got dinner at the Chatsworth farm store and ate at a picnic table in Pilsley—cold vegetable quiche and the best, softest strawberries I've ever had. Ours in the States are tough and vulgar by comparison.

Wouldn't you think that after thirty-some years of eating every day, three meals a day plus extra, you could take a couple of days off without consequences? I never actually realized how much I eat before I came over here. I always seem hungry at night when I go to bed because I don't have constant access to a refrigerator for my regular late-night bowl of cereal or ice cream.

Sandwiches are mostly bready things with the smallest amount of meat possible. At every opportunity they will put cucumbers on them. Or you can have something like cheese and onion, held together with mayonnaise. After a few days, I began to wonder how anyone gets enough protein in this country.

It's impossible to get a good cup of coffee. Most everyone considers coffee to be the powdered instant stuff and even that they manage to make weak. (Although, I started to almost like this in the evenings in my cozy little room in Bath.) Starbucks is the same, I suppose, but half-and-half does not even exist here and they don't put out cream, so you have to make do with milk. Even at a restaurant, if you attempt to order decaf, they'll bring you watery instant with milk. Blech.

I have always loved the idea of England, meaning that I watch a lot of BBC America, love Trinny and Susannah (well-known fashion gurus and journalists), and Bridget Jones, and Austen of course, and the idea of afternoon tea. Until this trip I couldn't tell an Earl Grey from a Lipton, and now I've become a bit of a tea snob because in America we just don't know how to make good tea, and after a month of not being able to get good coffee I can tell the difference. Also, one should never use cream in tea; it's far too rich. Or so they tell me. When I've been watching too much BBC America and too many costume dramas, the voice in my head (you know, the running commentary that goes on all day, or when you do something like imagine yourself as a guest on *Oprah* or *The Daily Show*—and should I be embarrassed to admit that? Perhaps it's a particular fault of writers, or maybe only writers with a great deal of pride)... Anyway, when I've been watching too much British stuff, that voice in my head actually has a British accent.

So sometimes I'm dismayed to find myself in a place that actually does feel foreign to me. There's a general coldness. Hotel staff and restaurant workers and people on the street can seem rude. They don't really want to know how you are; they just want to do their jobs. And to be honest, in America, we don't want to know how you are either really, but we're going to ask to make you feel like we are concerned and caring and open. Please just tell us you're okay, and then everyone can keep being happy and polite in this little social construct we've set up.

Sometimes I think people here find me too open. I asked questions the other night at the tour of the Roman Baths. It was a small group, and there were things I wanted to know—I don't even remember what now, but things like why don't they still use it and how high would the water have come in the King's Bath, which was open in Jane's day, just below the Pump Room. I really enjoyed it and got the sense that some of my British companions did not appreciate my open enthusiasm and would rather I'd just kept my mouth shut. But it's the Roman Baths for crying out loud. It was evening, and it was almost empty, and there were torches. How cool is that?

Mark and Gill said that when Gill's father came over to the U.S. and they were driving around the East Coast, he thought it was hysterical how even the tollbooth change-collectors asked him how he was. And he got to where he would ask them back and just laugh. Because in England, you would only ask someone that if you really knew them well—and really cared about the answer. And now I realize I've gone around England for a month smiling and asking people how they are.

I think that I am not entirely well. I mean, there are lots of ways in which any one of us could probably be said to be not well, but physically I think my body is not healthy.

I am tired too much—all the time. Today there's a hum of exhaustion under everything, louder than usual. I usually feel like I am pushing myself. I think people don't see it. But physically I am always on edge, always without reserves.

I push myself because I refuse not to, because I want to have a life.

I think the chocolate here is better. There is a convenience store across the street, and I'm going to get a Cadbury Flake on my way home. I will probably ask the salesclerk how she is. And tomorrow I'll wear my jeans for the fifteenth time since they were last washed, ride on the sticky leather seat of a cab, sit at a deserted train station that smells of urine, dragging my suitcase and overstuffed backpack through the grime and dirt of public transportation. I don't want to go home, and at the same time I do, and that's the rub of it all. Always.

⚜

Stoneleigh Abbey is lovely, a grand, white classical front that has been marred a little by smoke, with rows of windows looking out on a broad green lawn, with the slow River Avon running alongside. The house is built around an old abbey, so that one wing is completely "new" as of the early 1700s. Much of the rest dates back to the Tudor period, but there are parts of the twelfth-century abbey still in existence. Which makes it awfully similar to Northanger Abbey, where Catherine visits the Tilneys and is terribly discouraged to find so little of the original abbey left and so little in the way of romance and horror. I took the train here today on my way to Gill's cousin Niki's in London, and once again I have all of my suitcases and look like I am moving in.

This was the Leigh family's—Jane's mother's family's—ancestral home. Jane and her mother came to visit shortly after her father's death. The fifth Lord Leigh had died twenty years previously. He went mad apparently, left no heirs, and left the estate to his sister, but her recent death meant the inheritance of the estate was much in question. Jane and her mom went to visit her cousin, Thomas Leigh, who wanted to go to Stoneleigh to help make his claim for the estate. Mrs. Austen called the state bedroom—now a rather dark library—"an alarming apartment just fit for an Heroine,"[1] and it seems that it is similarly situated to the room that was the deceased Mrs. Tilney's in the book, which Catherine visits on her own, hoping to find a scandal, hoping to find the poor abused wife hidden away, being starved to death by her secretly cruel husband. Jane would have written *Northanger Abbey* long before she came to Stoneleigh, although she did revise it later.

Humphry Repton, already working on Thomas Leigh's estate in Adlestrop, did the grounds after Jane's visit, which they say to some extent model those of Sotherton Court in *Mansfield Park*. I couldn't remember the description enough to tell, and I didn't have time to explore. But Repton—possibly the most influential landscape gardener England ever produced[2]—is much discussed in *Mansfield Park* as the one Rushworth wants to get to improve Sotherton.

There is a simple chapel as well, which seems to fit the description of the one there, though Jane didn't go into great detail with it. Jane took a great deal of pride in making her characters up from scratch—she was certainly inspired by people she knew, but her creations were all her own. There are so many great houses that claim to have inspired her, but I imagine she probably invented country estates the way she invented people, though she may have taken pieces from one and pieces from another.

In the midst of all the other history and non-Austen information (like the tiny bathtub Queen Victoria used when she stayed here), I was struck by a picture in one of the parlors of a pretty woman named Elizabeth Wentworth with dark hair, kind eyes, and a gentle smile. It seems she was a friend of the family who came to visit for five days and ended up staying forty years. I immediately wondered if there was any connection to Captain Wentworth of *Persuasion*, and they told me Anne's story is actually based on her. I've never heard of her before, but they say that Betty Wentworth's maiden name was Betty Lord. As a young woman, she fell in love with a naval officer whom her mother forbid her to marry. But love won, and she married him anyway in secret. Not until years later, when she was being pressured to accept another suitor, was the whole thing revealed. Different from Anne, but perhaps this was Jane's inspiration. The timing would have been right since she wrote *Persuasion* well after her stay at Stoneleigh.

I heard writer Sue Monk Kidd talk once about the defining choice every woman makes between love and independence. There's no doubt in my mind right now what I would choose. I want to write, and I want to have a family. I want to go to grad school as well and travel and all other sorts of things, but if I have a chance at love, I would choose that. I know that now, at this moment in my life.

Some of us do get to make the choice between love and independence, but for many of us the choice simply happens—having found no one, having had no one find us, we land squarely and often surprisedly on the side of independence.

We may alternately long for it and turn from it, the question of the choice between independence and love not being a simple one, as it wasn't for Jane. We recognize the value of what we lose if we marry—and not merely the simple if significant ability to spend all of our time and money completely on ourselves, but the value of the completely self-directed life (although as a Christian I don't view my life as self-directed but God-directed, there is still an essential freedom here).

I love that freedom. And convolutedly long for someone to share it with. I long for someone to care about the quotidian things, to know about the daily turmoil and disruptions. I long for a sense of family. I find myself carrying on ten wonderful, in-depth discussions with ten excellent friends who rarely know one another, feeling incredibly grateful and incredibly stretched. So I long for someone to make a home with.

I long to be cherished.

And I realize that all marriages have their dark days—perhaps all come close to fissure at some point. I know that many women who choose love lose out on both scores, losing independence only to have love drain slowly away over the years. The longer I continue in my single life, the more determined I become that only something great could lure me away.

I wonder if Betty Lord's great love lasted, if it was worth her risk. How dashing was the real Captain Wentworth? Betty—and Jane as well—could only ever have limited independence, could never entirely get away from their families. So Betty chose love, against every prohibition, perhaps planting the grain of the story that would become dear Anne.

Twenty

Evensong

Give us Grace Almighty Father, so to pray,
as to deserve to be heard, to address thee with our
hearts, as with our lips. Thou art every where present.

—JANE AUSTEN, EVENING PRAYER I

I sat at the café at St. Mary's in Oxford, at the same table Jack and Spencer and I ate at on our last day there, eating the best omelet I have ever had—over toast, with a little balsamic vinegar on it, accompanied by a fresh salad with herbs. I was full of joy. I sat there outside just remembering, at this wooden table on the stone, watching the gray clouds over the dome of the Radcliffe Camera with the bright sun behind, praying the sun would win, and enjoying the weightiness of Oxford. Just as I sat there eating and drinking my almost-decent coffee, the sun did win. It stayed out all the rest of the day.

I went into the Ashmolean Museum, just for a few minutes, to see some sketches from da Vinci and Rembrandt, but I'm afraid I've lost all my patience with museums, so I walked down to Magdalen College again (once again, buying cigars en route) and sat in front of Lewis's

New Building to wait while they finished moving the college flock of deer so I could walk around quiet Addison's Walk. Big groups of people were out punting on the river in the sun—or, more accurately, trying to learn to punt—but the walk itself was almost empty. Jack said there was a wonderful view of the city here, but I couldn't find it and was too tired to look much and, honestly, too tired to do much thinking.

I walked the wide path all the way down the banks of the River Cherwell, manicured lawns on one side and manicured river on the other, with the occasional bevy of swans. I lay on the grass in the sun. I wanted to turn over again the things in my heart, every goodness from the trip, to prepare for whatever might meet me when I got home.

I went back to Christ Church Cathedral for Evensong. It seemed like a perfect little bookend for the end of the trip since that's how it began.

The choir was there. I was so glad. There is something about hearing the psalms sung as opposed to just having them read. I sat in a pew on the south side in the late afternoon light, facing one of the large stained-glass windows. My heart fully participated, in spite of my exhaustion—maybe in some ways because of my exhaustion. And then they started to sing, the glorious choir.

I didn't hear which psalm they were starting with, so I couldn't follow along, but the three they sang are closely familiar.

"The Lord is my light and my salvation," they sang, "whom shall I fear? The Lord is the stronghold of my life; of whom shall I be afraid?" (Psalm 27:1).

Yes, my heart responded. *Yes.*

There are so many uncertainties, but this I know. This is what I seek, to dwell in the house of the Lord, to gaze upon his beauty. He will keep me safe; he will shelter me and set me high upon a rock. He will hear my voice, be merciful to me, and answer me.

My heart says, Seek his face.

He will teach me his way and lead me in a straight path.

To the Lord I call, praying that he will not turn a deaf ear to me. If he is silent, it will be like death itself. He will hear my cry for mercy. I will lift up my hands.

The Lord is my strength and shield; my heart trusts in him, and I am helped. My heart leaps for joy.

Ascribe to the Lord glory and strength. Give him the glory due his name. The voice of the Lord thunders over the waters. The voice of the Lord is powerful. The voice of the Lord is majestic. He is enthroned forever.

I am confident of this, that I will see the goodness of the Lord in the land of the living. He will give me strength. He will give me peace.[1]

I do not know why, but I know these things more than anything else. They are dear to me, and in that moment in Christ Church Cathedral—with the stained glass and the choir and the prayers, the strong old hymns, all the blessings I have been lavished with and all the deep questions—I knew them to be true.

⁂

At thirty-nine thousand feet, somewhere south of Newfoundland, my pen exploded and I got ink on my jeans. It's truly a lost day. My eyes looked horrible—bloodshot and puffy—and I was beyond tired. I couldn't concentrate on anything for more than an hour, and that was a very bad, reading-incredibly-slowly kind of concentration. I could not abide the thought of a movie when I got on board, so I tried to read the new *Harry Potter* book but didn't have enough energy for that either. I slept a bit but kept waking up with that jarring, falling, jumpy sensation that comes from trying to sleep on an airplane and not being entirely sure you won't fall out of the sky as a result. I had some mini–panic attacks before lunch and knew that when you get this tired, fear overwhelms—irrational fears of very small things, like, *You want me to do what? You want me to eat lasagna? You want me to sit here in this metal tube hurtling through space while it fills up with dinner smells, people just eating and pretending that everything is normal?*

My psyche wasn't entirely capable of that, so I ate my lasagna in very small bites and prayed I wouldn't pass out or somehow fall through the bottom of the plane.

Heathrow was nightmarish. There were masses of people everywhere, everyone going in different directions, so that it was impossible to move anywhere in a straight line. My incredibly long check-in line included insane French circus people carrying stuffed animals, making loud chicken noises, and wearing various fake noses—one of which was made to look like a man's private anatomy—and generally making themselves as obnoxious as possible. And then there was the French couple behind me kissing passionately the entire time we were in line.

In that moment, completely exhausted, hungry, trying to manage my suitcase, my ridiculously heavy backpack, and a carrier bag full of odds and ends that was now beginning to rip, surrounded by a sea of humanity and annoying French circus kissing people, I came to several stark realizations:

1. I do not like French people.
2. I do not want anyone to kiss me. Ever.

3. I am sure that Jack has no intentions whatsoever, and how could I not have seen that before?

This is what I have come to know as my downward spiral. In such a descent, everything is bad, everything around me, and I cannot pull myself out of the emotional morass.

The airline didn't announce my gate for another hour then made a special point of noting that said gate was the absolute farthest one from the main terminal and that all passengers should be aware of the fifteen-minute walk. The air smelled like toast, which made me gag; even now I'm convinced that if there were a national smell in England, it would be the smell of toast. Forget English breakfasts, everyone eats charred white bread they've scraped with butter or maybe Marmite.

When I had finally checked my e-mail the night before, the late news was on. It had been nearly an entire week, which was killing me because the last time I'd been able to check was Saturday in Bath, so I was intrigued to find that I had an e-mail from some William Denby person with the subject line AUSTEN AND JORDAN.

I didn't recognize the name, but I thought it sounded legit, so I opened it and realized (duh) it was from Jack. I skimmed his note, and it seemed a bit formal and not quite what I hoped for, and I didn't want to discover that, so I left it. Instead I drank a glass of wine with Niki, Gill's cousin, whom I'd been staying with and told her all about Jack. We talked about how Christian guys can be weird and noncommittal and how she was dating someone who didn't go to church and wondered if maybe we really did have to go outside the church to find someone normal who actually wants a relationship. Niki told me it was, unfortunately, all the same in England.

When I was fuzzy from exhaustion, sometime around midnight, I went back and read Jack's e-mail. He asked a ton of questions (good), told me a little about Jordan (good), said he'd had a bit of a hard time adjusting at first in Jordan because he'd had such a good time in Oxford (good). Said we'd had such a "great crew" in Oxford (hmm…). Asked if maybe I would want to get together for lunch (lunch?!) when he got back from spending a week in North Carolina, where, he pointed out, he was seeing his new niece and going to his nephew's birthday party.

The e-mail felt chummy, or purposely distant, and far too formal. It lacked warmth. It lacked any sign of the intimacy we'd established. He even signed it with his whole name, though perhaps that is excusable in his case because of the potential of name confusion. He seemed not to remember that I would still be in England.

So, I thought, *overall pretty good, though perhaps not as good as I would like it to be.* He had written, he was interested in my trip, he sounded like maybe he missed me, and he did want to see me even if only for lunch.

I wrote back and told him tiny bits about the trip, told him I "so enjoyed hanging out with him in Oxford," would love to do lunch, but would he rather come over for brunch or dinner sometime?

Then I went to sleep.

When I checked my e-mail the next morning, there was nothing. Standing in line at Heathrow, I was determined that Jack must have been going to North Carolina to see that girl he was dating, and the questions began spinning. *Why else would he need a whole week to see his new niece and go to his nephew's birthday party? If he were really into me, why would he send an e-mail instead of calling? Did he assume I wasn't in England anymore? Why would he only want to do lunch? He might as well just come out and say he's not interested. Argh!*

Perhaps my perspective was a bit skewed, as I was apparently disgusted with all of humanity (especially male-anatomy-nose-wearing French circus people). Perhaps I could wait to see what he says in the next e-mail before entirely giving up hope. I was nearly determined, however, that he was one of those horrible Christian guys who would never know what he wanted or would never step up to the plate to make it happen. I couldn't abide that, and I suppose I would have no reason to abide that as no initiative would be taken and nothing would ever happen.

After the day in Oxford, facing the possibility that this was all rubbish (and laughing at myself at the same time for thinking it is rubbish because he e-mailed me and wanted to get together for lunch), I felt the reassurance of warm, very good memories of this trip even if all of this fell through. And that calm moment at Evensong, in the intensity of hearing the choir sing, "…of whom shall I be afraid?" I believed that.

I still do.

So Oxford was my own again; sometime during my walk by the river, I believed I could love it simply for my own sake without always tying it to memories of Jack.

Niki took me grocery shopping, and I bought two large tins of golden syrup for making treacle tart and a huge thing of Marmite for Gill, which I have since decided was a very bad idea, and I have vowed I will never buy anything heavy again when I travel. Directly south of St. John, with just 650 miles left till landing in D.C., I was especially thankful for the sun in Oxford, even though my pen kept leaking and my fingers were now black like Jo March's in *Little Women*.

The Return to Ordinary

There is mercy in every place;
And mercy, encouraging thought!
Gives even affliction a grace.

—WILLIAM COWPER

One thing I love about Austen's books as opposed to the movies is that she tells us a little more about how the characters' lives turn out. The movies tend to end with a wedding, and that's that, as though there is nothing more worth telling. But in the books we learn, for instance, that Wickham was never allowed to visit Pemberley, that Darcy and Bingley continued to be great friends and their wives the closest of sisters, that they all helped to contribute to Lydia's upkeep but Lydia never felt that she was given enough. We know that Elinor and Edward were quite content in the Delaford parsonage after they redecorated everything and that Lady Russell and Captain Wentworth forgave each other and put their differences aside.

Among the small things I want to tell you is how I've developed an addiction to English tea—always with milk, of course, never with half-and-half, like a good little Anglophile. I've almost given up coffee altogether.

I have a new niece—Sweet Isa, my brother and sister-in-law's daughter. She has my eyes. Or rather, she has my brother's eyes with my sister-in-law's coloring, and she looks a little like me. She has a way of looking very seriously at the world when there is not a grin on her face. On the night she was born, I drove to the hospital and could almost feel my world changing for hers, the circle of life and all. Perhaps it is inappropriate to think about death on the night a baby is born, but that is what it made me think, how all of us only overlap for such a short period of time really.

I miss the monks. A necklace I made in Bath—silver and pale pink beads on a black cord, with a cross I bought at the abbey—is one of my favorite things. I have even, from time to time, made cheese and onion sandwiches. On the first morning I got home, I woke up at five thirty and put in a CD I got at Magdalen College on my last day in Oxford— "Oh be joyful in the Lord all ye lands," it begins, the "Jubilate Deo" of the *Book of Common Prayer* and Psalm 100—and just lay there in the sun remembering, full of every goodness.

I suppose you will want to know the end of my story with Jack.

In spite of my doubts at Heathrow, I came home glowing. Partly because of just being in England I'm sure, but largely because of Jack. My friends knew I had met someone before I told them just by the look on my face. I was deeply happy and incredibly pleased with the world.

I think maybe love always dies, so maybe we shouldn't be surprised by this. I don't mean genuine love, the *agape* or *phileo* love New Testament writers describe. Because genuine love isn't really feelings, not the thing that makes the entire world seem far more fascinating, everything funnier and brighter and more interesting than before. It is that at the beginning, and then that fades and life takes on a more normal hue.

In the best cases, maybe the feelings come and go, and you can expect to revisit them frequently over the course of a relationship, or maybe they continue in a deeper if slightly less urgent form. I don't know. Maybe I know very little about it at all really.

The feelings between Jack and me died a long and torturous death. At least mine did. I never really ascertained what his were. From my perspective, it seems that they could have been quickly and cleanly put out of their misery with one honest admission on his part. He chose instead to sort of leave them out in the cold on their own to see if they might be able to survive. Eventually they starved to death.

It was a little more than a week after I got home before I heard from him. He wanted to do lunch, which I thought was a sure sign that he was going to break bad news. So I put on my jeans and ironed my hip little black sleeveless shirt and put on my favorite garnet earrings and necklace and left for the Town Center. I'm sure I looked like the nervous wreck I was. I'd had a month to imagine him as the most perfect man I ever met, and this was where those dreams would hit reality.

It was all a bit awkward. He had copies of the pictures of us together from Oxford, but I didn't know what to say about them because I had no idea what they meant. At the end, after I had picked through my salad, he opened up about his state of mind.

He was overwhelmed. School was starting again, and he wasn't sure about how he was going to pay the bills, or exactly what he wanted to do after he graduated. He wasn't sure he'd be able to stay in school full time. He said he needed time to figure out things. I was determined to be patient and understanding, not to pressure him, so I just tried to be supportive and didn't ask the questions I should have—like, "What does this mean for us?" and, "Are you still seeing the girl in North Carolina?"

I didn't want to push, so all those things were left under the surface. I heard him asking for time; I backed off.

I told myself, *He doesn't owe me anything. I don't want to add stress to his life. I want him to call me when he feels like calling me, get together if he feels like getting together.* And part of me still knew it would all work out. This was just a little delay.

I trusted him to tell me if he was still dating the North Carolina girl. He'd been so open about her before that I didn't think he had reason to hide anything. So we left and he said something like, "I'll be in touch." And I believed him. I went home and began waiting—waiting for him to get his life figured out, waiting for him to find paying work, waiting for him to make time for me.

All of my nice, reassuring, mature internal dialogue quickly devolved into *Why haven't I heard from him?*

A month was enough to break my heart, or to place me squarely in limbo, which is officially worse than a broken heart. I could give you all the lurid details (not that any of them are actually lurid): the waiting for e-mails, the horrible not knowing, the hating him and loving him and being patient with him and finally giving up.

I moved on and started going out with other guys almost immediately—lots of other guys, actually, by my standards. I didn't really want to just sit around and wait for Jack and didn't particularly want to be readily available when he suddenly decided that he'd made a mistake and couldn't afford to let me go. Getting your heart to move on is another matter though. I was sad to have lost his friendship, to feel like I had made this great friend and lost him just as quickly, sad that we never explored what might have been. And no one else I met was very captivating.

❦

We met for coffee in October at my favorite place. I wore my brown T-shirt and long jeans with my three-inch spiked boots and plum corduroy jacket. I was running a low-grade fever, as I had been for weeks; the half of my face that was getting blasted by the heater flushed a bright red.

When we met, everything was stilted, with none of the familiarity we'd shared in Oxford. Eventually, staring at the floor, the table, and his tea, Jack said, "So I wanted to let you know, I, uh, have continued to keep in contact with that person in North Carolina."

I froze. I didn't want to be angry, but I was. I wanted to ask, "Does she know you call her 'that person in North Carolina'?" But I was afraid of what I might blurt out, so I didn't say anything.

There were other meetings, more intense, and very honest conversations—things that got my heart riled up at various points over the following months. But, and maybe this could have been predicted, Jack never pursued me.

Eventually, with time, his change of heart became to everyone's satisfaction, including my own. I confess to crafting a little speech à la Elizabeth Bennet so that, when he came back, I could tell him precisely why I wasn't interested. But he didn't come back, and as much as I'd like to characterize him as one of *those* Christian guys—the kind who just don't commit, who are still growing up at forty—I could only really conclude that he wasn't interested *enough*.

As Mr. Collins would attest, those we love necessarily begin to lose their value in our eyes when they don't return our affection, and such was the case with Jack. The more I thought about what happened, if I held it in my mind a certain way, I could see weaknesses and incompatibilities, at least enough to make me content.

So the adoration went away, and the anger went away too.

My life returned to stasis, but with a new understanding of the kind of companionship that's possible and with a hope of finding someone who wants that kind of dear friendship, to the kind you don't, *won't,* just throw away.

In the meantime, something else was happening in my life of greater significance.

By October, a couple months after getting back, I could no longer pretend to be healthy. My body plummeted into another round of debilitating exhaustion. I was tired all the time. I couldn't sleep well— couldn't rest—and could only work for four hours or so, and this was on the good days.

By November, I'd resigned myself to another round of doctor visits. My family doctor said my face looked a little funny, asked if I had ever had Bell's palsy, and then said, "It will probably always be a mystery why you feel bad."

So when the infectious-disease specialist also could find nothing wrong, I cried and went to see a chronic-fatigue specialist, beginning to resign myself to the fate of a strange illness no one understood.

To my great relief, in March I was diagnosed.

Lyme disease.

All the exhaustion, all the fatigue, all the brain fog and struggling to keep up with life for the last six years suddenly had a name; it had all been due to a tiny deer tick that infected me with the *Borrelia burgdor-feri* bacteria when I was backpacking or in the country picking berries with a friend. For years it thrived, wreaking havoc with my life, even throwing off my autonomic nervous functions, my heart rate, and my breathing. It turned out that most people never know they've been bitten by a tick, and I was one of them. I'd had a small ring on my leg that I thought was a spider bite. So I slipped through the cracks. For years.

The intervening six months are slightly fuzzy. But I remember going to church in tears, overwhelmed at the grace of just having a name for this illness—a name that wasn't laziness or lack of motivation—and to think there was a bacteria alive inside my body, something we could fight and hopefully kill, to think that maybe I could be healthy again. This idea was like seeing the heavens open and having God offer me back my life, a gift I'd given up hoping for. The truth is I'd given up praying for actual healing. I'd only been praying for a doctor who would be able to help me manage whatever this illness was. So I went to the altar, and a man named Joe prayed with me and anointed me with oil, and I cried.

And then I plunged into a darkness I never expected, brought on by the antibiotics fighting the bacteria in my body.

My days became very, very small. For weeks all I could do was lie on the couch and rest or mindlessly watch TV and then go to bed at night, in my very quiet house, in my empty bed, where I still couldn't sleep. I felt like someone was holding my head under water, and I could do nothing about it. I felt like I was living in the shadow of death.

In fact, death began to look attractive again.

I developed strong feelings for my butcher knife—I wanted to have it close to me and lie down with it against my cheek on the kitchen floor and keep it under my pillow at night. Once I woke up around 3:00 a.m., rocking and sobbing on my bed with exhaustion and the strongest desire to destroy everything I could touch. I wanted to cut off my hair and cut up my clothes and my sheets and curtains and shower curtain.

I talked myself out of it with a great deal of effort because I thought if my mother found me with ragged hair, holding scissors, sitting in a pile of scraps that used to be my clothes, she would take me to the hospital; I didn't really think isolation in a psych ward would be much fun.

I began to read Job, and finally I understood why the first thing he did in the midst of despair was to shave his head and tear his clothes.

Here, gently, carefully, I was brought face-to-face with the grace of God in ways I never expected and, without this experience, could never have understood. I have sometimes been surprised to meet grace here, though perhaps I shouldn't be. "Yea, though I walk through the valley of the shadow of death, I will fear no evil," the psalmist says, "for thou art with me; thy rod and thy staff they comfort me" (Psalm 23:4, KJV).

I should tell you though that I don't say this as a particularly cheerful Christian. I understand now that living through lamentation is part of life's process and should not be run from or avoided, so I have no desire to stuff all these things away and try to make them artificially bright...because there have been weeks when I felt so incredibly alone that I wondered if God was with me anymore. Once, when it was particularly bad, after the waking in the middle of the night and wanting to destroy my life thing, my friend Leigh held my hands and looked me in the eye and said, "You are not forsaken, Lori. You are not forsaken." Then she prayed over me loudly and cried for me.

And she was right.

I wasn't and am not forsaken. And this is where my walk with Jane comes in again, because Jane taught me something about the value of an ordinary life—things I'm not sure I could understand before I was stripped of being able to do even the ordinary. She did not want to be famous. She wanted to love her family and her friends, to live her faith rather than talk about it, to do good work and tell good stories.

She enjoyed making money with her writing and even developed a little jealousy, like any good writer. She felt that Sir Walter Scott should have been content enough with his success in poetry without venturing into fiction. "Walter Scott has no business to write novels, especially good ones," she joked. "It is not fair.—He has Fame & Profit enough as a Poet, and should not be taking the bread out of other people's mouths."[1] I don't think she ever knew that he owned several well-worn copies of her books.[2]

And while Jane was—*is*—big, she never believed that being big was important.

These are the things I want for myself, the things that became more important after my own dark night where I learned that there's no end to the grace of God—where it was big enough for every single day that I got up and could do nothing. It didn't matter if I could never write again, if I could never work again. God does not love me because of anything I can do; this still astonishes me. He simply loves me. Me, me, me. Sitting on the couch or sobbing or staring vegetatively at the TV.

All my life I've been taught to rely on the grace of God, and yet in practice I've tried to earn his love, and my own significance, by running and doing. So it has been a measure of grace to not be able to run any longer, to simply be forced to...be.

And this is the paradox, because this life—this loving your family and friends and doing good work and telling good stories life—may feel small, but it is far from ordinary.

It is the best life, the extraordinary life.

It was Jane's, and I hope it will be mine.

⚜

Austen told her family even more about the way her stories ended, what happened to her characters over time. She told them that *Pride and Prejudice*'s Mary Bennet did eventually marry (one of her uncle Phillips's clerks), that Emma and Mr. Knightley lived at Hartfield only for a couple years before Mr. Woodhouse's health failed; that *Persuasion*'s silly Miss Steele never did manage to catch her dear doctor.

As for my own story, who can tell?

My days are still small. But the light is beginning to return. Just a couple weeks ago I started being able to laugh at the world again, and that felt very good—soul-healing laughter. I want more of it, to enjoy life, to love the people around me.

I feel incredibly blessed to be in such a family, with dear friends, with the prospect of work that I love, living a small life surrounded by small goodnesses with this tremendous grace.

I hope I will be healthy again.

I believe I will go back to England, to visit or maybe to study.

Margaret said when I was there, "Why couldn't you meet a nice English boy?"

And perhaps I will. Maybe I will have the good fortune to find something like a poor, earnest country curate, a modern-day Mr. Collins in the flesh.

Like Lizzy—or more to the point, like Jane—I'm determined to marry only for love, so perhaps I will end an old maid and teach my nieces to play the piano very ill.

In the future I'll put more weight in someone's words than in the look in his eyes. I know now that I could have been stronger with Jack. I should have asked him to be clearer. I see how looks cannot always be trusted, however Darcy-ish they may be.

On the other hand, I have no regrets. I felt something for Jack and stepped out of my fear and just went with it.

I am proud of that. I tried.

And I think I will try again.

Acknowledgments

This book was written during a year I would not have survived without the endless care of my parents, the support of my dear friends Catherine Claire and Kristine Steakley, and the prayers and kindness of so many others. I am so grateful for all their love.

I want to thank those who helped me on this trip: Gill and Mark Kalbskopf, who helped me plan; Margaret Noel, who welcomed me into her home; Christine and David Blower; Phil and Sue Howe of Hidden Britain Tours, who found me at Deane and enabled me to get into St. Nicholas in Steventon; "Susan" for driving me all around Hampshire; the monks at Alton Abbey; Rod and Jo Spenseley at the Devonshire Arms in Pilsley; the staff at the Chawton House Library, who allowed me to spend a wonderful day there doing decidedly non-scholarly research; and especially "William" the cabby, who rescued me from the shoulder of an A road in Kent.

I also want to thank my wonderful agent, Beth Jusino, and my editor, Jeanette Thomason, who has a Jane Austen action figure on her desk and championed this project from the very beginning.

The Works of Jane Austen

Sense and Sensibility (1811)
Pride and Prejudice (1813)
Mansfield Park (1814)
Emma (1815)
Northanger Abbey (1817)
Persuasion (1817)
Sanditon (written in 1817, but unfinished)

Bibliography

Austen, Jane. *Catharine and Other Writings*. Edited by Margaret Anne Doody and Douglas Murray. New York: Oxford University Press, 1998.

——. *Emma*. New York: Signet Classic, 1980.

——. *Lady Susan, The Watsons, Sanditon*. New York: Penguin Putnam, 2003.

——. *Mansfield Park*. New York: Oxford University Press, 2003.

——. *Northanger Abbey*. New York: Penguin Books, 1985.

——. *Persuasion*. New York: Penguin Books, 1994.

——. *Pride and Prejudice*. New York: Signet Classic, 1980.

——. *Sense and Sensibility*. New York: Bantam Books, 1983.

Austen-Leigh, J. E., *A Memoir of Jane Austen and Other Family Recollections*. Edited by Kathryn Sutherland. New York: Oxford University Press, 2002.

Cowper, William. *Selected Poems*. New York: Routledge, 2003.

Edwards, Anne-Marie, *In the Steps of Jane Austen: Walking Tours of Austen's England*. Madison, WI: Jones Books, 2003.

Le Faye, Deirdre. *A Chronology of Jane Austen and Her Family*. New York: Cambridge University Press, 2006.

——. *Jane Austen: A Family Record*. New York: Cambridge University Press, 2004.

——. *Jane Austen: The World of Her Novels*. New York: Harry N. Abrams, 2002.

——, ed. *Jane Austen's Letters*. New York: Oxford University Press, 1997. All excerpts from *Jane Austen's Letters,* collected and edited by Deirdre Le Faye, reprinted with permission of Oxford University Press.

————. *Jane Austen's 'Outlandish Cousin': The Life and Letters of Eliza de Feuillide.* London: The British Library, 2002.

Leapman, Michael, main contributor. *Eyewitness Travel Guides Great Britain.* New York: DK Publishing, 2005.

Lewis, C. S., *Selected Literary Essays.* New York: Cambridge University Press, 1969.

Moorman, John R. H. *A History of the Church in England.* Harrisburg, PA: Morehouse, 1980.

Ray, Joan Klingel. *Jane Austen for Dummies.* Hoboken, NJ: Wiley, 2006.

Shields, Carol. *Jane Austen.* New York: Viking Penguin, 2001.

Tomalin, Claire. *Jane Austen: A Life.* New York: Vintage Books, 1999.

Notes

A Note on the Text

The epigraph is drawn from Austen, *Lady Susan, The Watsons, Sanditon,* 166.

Introduction: Loving Austen

The epigraph is drawn from Austen, *Northanger Abbey,* 40.

1. Le Faye, *Family Record,* xix.
2. Le Faye, *Family Record,* 12.
3. Le Faye, *Family Record,* 13.
4. Tomalin, *A Life,* 7.
5 Austen-Leigh, *A Memoir,* 141.
6. Austen-Leigh, 29.

Chapter 1: Crossing Oceans

The epigraph is drawn from Le Faye, *Letters,* 29.

1. Le Faye, *Family Record,* 11.
2. Le Faye, *Family Record,* 4.
3. Le Faye, *Family Record,* 12.
4. Le Faye, *Family Record,* 3–4.
5. Le Faye, *Family Record,* 272.
6. C. S. Lewis, *Selected Literary Essays,* 185.

7. Austen, *Love and Freindship* [sic], (London: Chatto & Windus, 1922), xiv–xv.

8. Austen-Leigh, 70. Tomalin, 181.

Chapter 2: Oxford: Dirt and Dreaming

The epigraph is drawn from Austen, *Pride and Prejudice,* 186.

1. Le Faye, *Family Record,* 47.

2. Austen-Leigh, 160.

3. Le Faye, *Family Record,* 7.

Chapter 3: Christ Church: Good Company

The epigraph is drawn from Austen, *Sense and Sensibility,* 14.

1. Austen-Leigh, 79–80.

2. Austen-Leigh, 160.

3. Austen, *Persuasion,* 243.

4. Austen, *Emma,* 294.

5. Austen, *Pride and Prejudice,* 310.

6. Austen, *Sense and Sensibility,* 331.

7. Austen, *Pride and Prejudice,* 261.

8. C. S. Lewis, *Selected Literary Essays,* (New York: Cambridge University Press, 1969), 185.

9. Austen, *Catharine and Other Writings,* 247.

10. Austen, *Persuasion,* 148.

11. Austen, *Pride and Prejudice,* 14.

Chapter 4: Austenian Faith and Love

The epigraph is drawn from Cowper, *Selected Poems,* 36. Cowper was Jane's favorite poet.

1. Le Faye, *Letters,* 322.

2. Le Faye, *Letters,* 148.

3. Le Faye, *Family Record,* 233.

4. Le Faye, *Letters,* 280.

Chapter 5: Alarms (Fire and Otherwise)
The epigraph is drawn from Austen, *Northanger Abbey,* 106.
1. Austen-Leigh, 119.
2. Le Faye, *Family Record,* 270.
3. Le Faye, *Letters,* 1.
4. Le Faye, *Letters,* 2.
5. Le Faye, *Letters,* 3.
6. Tomalin, 119.
7. Le Faye, *Family Record,* 92–94.
8. Tomalin 120. Le Faye says Lefroy went on to have nine children (*Letters,* 545), but other sources also put the number at seven.
9. Le Faye, *Letters,* 4.
10. Leapman, *Eyewitness Travel Guides Great Britain,* 214.
11. Le Faye, *Family Record,* 106.
12. Le Faye, *Letters,* 216.
13. Le Faye, *Letters,* 19.
14. Le Faye, *Family Record,* 137.
15. Tomalin, 179–80.
16. Le Faye, *Family Record,* 138.
17. Le Faye, *Family Record,* 143.

Chapter 6: Simple Conversation
The epigraph is drawn from Austen, *Pride and Prejudice,* 9.

Chapter 7: Alton Abbey: Incense and Blooms
The epigraph is drawn from Austen, *Pride and Prejudice,* 25.
1. James Wright, "A Blessing," in *Above the River: The Complete Poems,* (Middletown, CT: Wesleyan University Press, 1990), 143.

2. Austen, *Sense and Sensibility,* 158.

3. Le Faye, *Family Record,* 92, 101 and Tomalin, 106, 124.

4. Le Faye, *Outlandish Cousin,* 138.

5. Le Faye, *Letters,* 344.

Chapter 8: Steventon: A Solitary Walk
The epigraph is drawn from Austen, *Pride and Prejudice,* 32.

1. Le Faye, *Family Record,* 13.

2. Le Faye, *Family Record,* 13, 128.

3. Tomalin, 4.

4. Austen, *Northanger Abbey,* 38.

5. Le Faye, *Letters,* 57.

6. Le Faye, *Letters,* 275.

7. Austen, *Pride and Prejudice,* 32.

8. Edwards, *Steps of Jane Austen,* 35.

9. Le Faye, *Family Record,* 23.

10. Le Faye, *Letters,* 486.

11. Le Faye, *Family Record,* 4.

12. Le Faye, *Family Record,* 4.

13. Le Faye, *Family Record,* 21.

14. Le Faye, *Family Record,* 17.

15. Le Faye, *Family Record,* 20.

16. Le Faye, *Family Record,* 99.

17. Le Faye, *Family Record,* 41.

18. Le Faye, *Family Record,* 22.

19. Austen, *Mansfield Park,* 183.

20. Le Faye, *Outlandish Cousin,* 116.

21. Fanny Caroline Lefroy Family History, as quoted in Le Faye, *Family Record,* 105.

22. Austen-Leigh, 19.

23. Austen, *Pride and Prejudice,* 30.

24. Edwards, 35.

25. Edwards, 36.

26. C. S. Lewis, *Mere Christianity,* (New York: HarperSanFrancisco, 2001), 92.

27. Edwards, 39.

28. Le Faye, *Family Record,* 47.

29. Austen, *Catharine and Other Writings,* 238.

30. Austen, *Catharine and Other Writings,* 239.

Chapter 9: Chawton: Love and Grit

The epigraph is drawn from Austen, *Pride and Prejudice,* 130.

1. Le Faye, *Letters,* 201.

2. Le Faye, *Family Record,* 188.

3. Le Faye, *Letters,* 91.

4. Le Faye, *Family Record,* 17 and Tomalin, 28.

5. Le Faye, *Family Record,* 87.

6. Le Faye, *Family Record,* 43.

7. Le Faye, *Family Record,* 192.

8. Le Faye, *Family Record,* 55.

9. Le Faye, *Family Record,* 111.

10. Tomalin, 144–45.

11. Le Faye, *Family Record,* 234.

12. Austen, *Catharine and Other Writing,* 249–50.

13. Le Faye, *Family Record,* 211.

14. Edwards, 24.

15. Le Faye, *Letters,* 224.

Chapter 10: London: To Friends

The epigraph is drawn from Austen, *Northanger Abbey,* 54.

1. Austen, *Emma,* 294.

2. Austen, *Emma*, 294.

3. Austen, *Emma*, 294.

4. Austen, *Emma*, 297–98.

5. Le Faye, *Letters*, 17.

6. Le Faye, *Letters*, 86.

7. Austen, *Emma*, 231.

Chapter 11: The British Library

The epigraph is drawn from Le Faye, *Letters*, 191. Jane was referring to a recent battle.

1. Le Faye, *Letters*, 20.

2. Le Faye, *Family Record*, 7.

3. Le Faye, *Family Record*, 151.

4. Le Faye, *Family Record*, 125.

5. Le Faye, *Letters*, 323.

6. Madeleine L'Engle, *A Circle of Quiet*, (New York: HarperSanFrancisco, 1972), 21.

Chapter 12: On Beauty

The epigraph is drawn from Austen, *Northanger Abbey*, 43.

1. Austen-Leigh, 169.

2. Austen-Leigh, 158.

3. Le Faye, *A Family Record*, 141.

4. Austen, *Pride and Prejudice*, 6.

5. Austen, *Emma*, 5.

6. Austen, *Persuasion*, 4.

7. Austen, *Sense and Sensibility*, 39.

8. Austen, *Sense and Sensibility*, 39–40.

9. Austen, *Sense and Sensibility*, 4.

10. Le Faye, *Family Record*, 37.

11. Le Faye, *Family Record*, 37.
12. Le Faye, *Family Record*, 77.
13. Le Faye, *Family Record*, 105.
14. Le Faye, *Letters*, 215.
15. Le Faye, *Family Record*, 213.

Chapter 13: An A Road in Kent
The epigraph is drawn from Austen, *Sense and Sensibility*, 35.
1. Tomalin, 205.
2. Austen-Leigh, 158.

Chapter 14: Winchester: A Patient Descent
The epigraph is drawn from Le Faye, *Letters*, 344.
1. Le Faye, *Family Record*, 248.
2. Le Faye, *Family Record*, 251.
3. Le Faye, *Letters*, 344.
4. Le Faye, *Letters*, 30, 16, 27.
5. Le Faye, *Family Record*, 265; *Letters*, 489. (Anna says he was seventy-one, but if you do the math he was actually seventy-three.)
6. Le Faye, *Family Record*, 266.
7. Le Faye, *Letters*, 487.
8. Le Faye, *Family Record*, 236.
9. Le Faye, *Letters*, 326.
10. Le Faye, *Letters*, 336.
11. Le Faye, *Family Record*, 216–17.
12. Le Faye, *Family Record*, 234.
13. Le Faye, *Family Record*, 234.
14. Le Faye, *Family Record*, 246.
15. Le Faye, *Family Record*, 140.
16. Le Faye, *Letters*, 231.

17. Le Faye, *Letters,* 341.

18. Le Faye, *Letters,* 344, 347.

19. Wendell Berry, "The Wish to Be Generous," in *The Selected Poems of Wendell Berry,* (Washington, D.C.: Counterpoint, 1998), 70.

20. From the epitaph on Jane Austen's grave.

Chapter 15: Lyme: the Comforting Ocean

The epigraph is drawn from Austen, *Pride and Prejudice,* 194.

1. Austen, *Persuasion,* 94.

2. Austen, *Persuasion,* 94–5.

3. Le Faye, *Family Record,* 142.

4. Le Faye, *Letters,* 203.

5. Austen, *Persuasion,* 159.

Chapter 16: Sensibility and Self-Expression

The epigraph is drawn from Austen, *Persuasion,* 247.

1. *Persuasion* movie, BBC, 1995.

2. Austen, *Sense and Sensibility,* 313.

3. Austen, *Sense and Sensibility,* 4.

4. Le Faye, *Family Record,* 128.

5. Le Faye, *Family Record,* 10.

6. Le Faye, *Letters,* 68.

7. Austen-Leigh, 125.

8. Le Faye, *Family Record,* 144.

9. Le Faye, *Letters,* 85, 88.

10. Le Faye, *Letters,* 138.

11. Austen, *Persuasion,* 155.

12. Le Faye, *Letters,* 42.

13. Bath Preservation Trust, www.bath-preservation-trust.org.uk/museums/no1/ (accessed June 5, 2007).

14. Le Faye, *Family Record,* 135.

15. Austen, *Persuasion,* 183–84.

Chapter 17: The Bath Bun
The epigraph is drawn from Austen, *Northanger Abbey,* 199.

1. Austen, *Northanger Abbey,* 126.

2. Austen, *Northanger Abbey,* 240.

3. Austen, *Persuasion,* 233.

4. I thought this idea came from C.S. Lewis, but I've not been able to find it. It's possible I've stolen it from him—or maybe just from conversations with my roommate about him—but I've been unable to find the source.

5. Austen, *Northanger Abbey,* 202.

6. Le Faye, *Letters,* 486.

7. Le Faye, *Family Record,* 145.

8. Le Faye, *Letters,* 96.

9. Le Faye, *Letters,* 96.

10. Le Faye, *Letters,* 97.

11. Le Faye, *Letters,* xviii.

12. LeFaye, *Family Record,* 65 and Tomalin, 29, 61.

13. Austen, *Mansfield Park,* 74.

14. Austen, *Catharine and Other Writings,* 249–50.

15. William Shakespeare, "Much Ado About Nothing: Act 2, Scene 3," The Complete Works of William Shakespeare, operated by *The Tech,* http://shakespeare.mit.edu/much_ado/much_ado.2.3.html (accessed June 5, 2007).

Chapter 18: Pilsley and Pemberley (Or What Makes Darcy Great)
The epigraph is drawn from Austen, *Mansfield Park,* 3.

1. Austen, *Pride and Prejudice,* 208.

2. Le Faye, *Letters,* 280.

3. Genesis 3:16.

4. Le Faye, *Family Record*, 4–5, 18, 29–36 and Tomalin, 16–22.

5. Le Faye, *World of Her Novels*, 31.

6. Austen, *Pride and Prejudice*, 204.

7. Austen, *Pride and Prejudice*, 205.

Chapter 19: Over Hill and Dale

The epigraph is drawn from Austen, *Pride and Prejudice*, 99.

1. Le Faye, *Family Record*, 157.

2. Stephen Daniels, "Repton, Humphry (1752-1818)," *Oxford Dictionary of National Biography*, Oxford University Press, 2004. www.oxforddnb.com/view/article/23387, accessed 25 June 2007

Chapter 20: Evensong

The epigraph is drawn from Austen, Evening Prayer 1, *Catharine and Other Writing*, 247.

1. Paraphrase of Psalm 27.

One Year Later: The Return to Ordinary

The epigraph is drawn from Cowper, "Verses Supposed to be Written by Alexander Selkirk, During his Solitary Abode in the Island of Juan Fernandez (1782)," 40.

1. Le Faye, *Letters*, 277.

2. Austen-Leigh, 113.

Guide

A Walk with Jane Austen
Lori Smith

1. Lori would never call herself obsessed with Jane Austen, and yet how fine do you see the line between affinity and obsession (and where is that line for you)? For whom or what would you cross an ocean to better know and understand—and why?

2. What discoveries about Jane Austen are you relishing most that you found by going via Lori's travels to the places Jane loved and lived?

3. Lori and Jane have so much in common and are alike in so many ways. How are they different?

4. How might Lori and Jane be different were they born in the other's era or lifetime (and country)? Perhaps, dear reader, this seems obvious, but isn't it delicious to discuss?

5. What do you make of Lori's list for the perfect man (see chapter 3)? How like or unlike is this to Jane's list, written between the lines in her novels?

6. What "small meannesses" did Jane write into her novels? Where do you find those in Lori's story? Are "small meannesses" different today than in Jane's day two hundred years ago? How or how not?

7. In chapter 14, what do you make of Lori's understanding of

heaven and her take on what we, like Jane, leave behind us
when we die?

8. Jane Austen created so many characters in her novels (not the
least of which are the Dashwoods in *Sense and Sensibility*) who
struggled with the tug between selfishness and self-expression.
How does this show up in Lori's story? How is this a common
theme in most Austen literature? When are Jane's characters virtuous in self-expression without selfishness? Where do you find
this in Lori's journey as well?

9. Had it been you, trekking to Oxford, slogging book-filled luggage across the English countryside, wandering the courtyards
of abbeys, and sitting through Evensong in Christ Church
Cathedral, would you have explored Jane's life differently?
Where would you wish to start and end?

10. Looking back on Lori's journey, how do you think she found
(or not) what she went looking for in the footsteps of Jane?

About the Author

LORI SMITH is a freelance writer and a member of the Jane Austen Society of North America. Her writing has appeared in *Washington Post Book World*, *Publishers Weekly*, *Washingtonian* magazine, *BreakPoint Online*, *Discipleship Journal*, and *Today's Christian Woman*. Her first book, *The Single Truth*, approached singleness thoughtfully from a Christian perspective. She lives in the Virginia suburbs of Washington, D.C., where she takes ballet, drinks tea, and runs the Jane Austen Quote of the Day blog at www.austenquotes.com. You'll also find her at her blog for this book (or "blook") at www.followingausten.com. Her next big life goal is to adopt a dog and to return to England.